Getting on
Top of Your
Troubles

GETTING ON TOP OF YOUR TROUBLES

CHARLES A. TRENTHAM

BROADMAN PRESS
Nashville, Tennessee

Dewey Decimal Classification Number: 252
Library of Congress Catalog Card Number: 66–15151
Printed in the United States of America
5.N65KSP

To my mother and father
who stayed on top of a lot of trouble

Preface

It was in the winter of 1950 that I first met Dr. Leslie Weatherhead. He was in the common room at the University of Edinburgh to tell the theological students about his ministry among the bombarded people of Britain during the London blitz. He was there to tell us how we might be the ministers of Christ in putting the maimed minds, broken bodies, and shattered souls of people back together. Afterwards, I heard him preach in old St. George's West, that bastion of the faith made memorable by the ministry of Alexander Whyte.

Under the spell of Dr. Weatherhead's ministry, I went away with a consuming desire to be able to bring the resources of the gospel to bear immediately upon our human needs. For twenty-six years I have served as a Christian minister. In that period, I have wished many times for a book which I might hand to the common man and say: "Read a certain chapter which deals specifically with your problem in plain, lucid language." I have wanted a book which will help people to get on top of their troubles, a book which honestly faces the truth that trouble is as much a part of life as life itself.

This book is the result of that desire.

The last chapter is addressed to preachers and is in substance one of the H. I. Hester Lectures on Preaching which I was privileged to deliver to the students at Midwestern Baptist Theological Seminary in 1961. This is an attempt to encourage pastoral preaching.

The other chapters are direct, simple sermons related to every man's human predicament and designed to help him get on top of his troubles.

My thanks are due and are gratefully given to Dr. Wade H. Boswell, a highly esteemed Christian psychiatrist in Knoxville, who read the manuscript and made many helpful suggestions, and to my faithful secretary, Mary Elizabeth Tyler, who typed the manuscript many times.

Contents

1

How Modern Are Your Morals?

1 Timothy 4:12

*Let no man despise thy youth; but
be thou an example of the believ-
ers, in word, in conversation, in
charity, in spirit, in faith, in purity.*

May I intrude into your privacy and ask you an
impertinent question: How modern are your morals? I ask
this because our age values modernity above all else. Our
greatest achievement, we are told, should be total liberation
from the past. And when I mention morals, of course, this is
a subject which now has to do solely with sex. Our society is
so saturated with eroticism that man is driven mad by what
J. B. Priestly has described as "that twanging of a single
nerve in the dark." We are learning that we cannot keep our
sanity if we insist on playing with the processes of God by
which human life is created.

While sitting in a clinic in Atlanta, I opened the January,
1963, issue of *Glamour* magazine to an article which strongly
insisted that if there is a case to be made for the older sex
ethics, it must be made quickly. The writer, who is thoroughly at home in the ways of young women's minds, is
Millicent McIntosh, headmistress of the Brierley School in
New York. She candidly faced such questions as this one:

1

Should girls who become pregnant be expelled from high school? She listened to and dealt with a college girl's confession on a radio program in New York that very few of the girls she knew were virgins.

This brought the question to every American home: Are we going to abandon the standards which the most thoughtful people have cherished for centuries?

Before you answer this question, let me remind you that chastity was the only new virtue that the Christian religion introduced into this world. When the apostle Paul talked to Christians about how members of the church should behave, he said that there are three areas in which we must be examples for others. We are to be examples in love, in loyalty, and in purity. Because Christians insisted so stringently on purity, Swinburne accused Christianity of robbing the world of its natural joy. Therefore he could write of Jesus: "Thou hast conquered, O pale Galilean, and the world has grown gray at thy breath."

Rules Are Needed

The world has always believed that life must be gay and sprightly and unrestrained if there is to be happiness. We cannot be vibrantly alive, we say, if we are to be fettered by those ancient shibboleths mumbled over us by our fathers, mumbled over them by their fathers. May I suggest that if this is our belief, we need to pause and look honestly at the truth that those who think chastity is an outworn virtue might be surprised to find that chastity is far more than a traditional or religious concept. It is a psychological necessity. It has been clinically established that a normal woman cannot have a love affair without a profound emotional involvement. A sensible, intelligent woman becomes so strongly involved that she will be deeply disturbed, perhaps permanently disturbed when this affair is broken, even if it is broken by mutual consent. Should she discover that her lover has not really cared for her as she has for him, permanent damage can be done to her self-respect and to her ability to trust others.

The old cliché that everybody has the right to be happy was expounded years ago in this country by Bertrand and Dora Russell. They meant by this the abandoning of the disciplined life for women, that women had the right to complete sexual freedom. This new philosophy was welcomed and embraced as an integral part of the liberation of womanhood. Today, however, there is an abundance of philosophical and psychological evidence that women are only made frantic by this kind of freedom. Not even the adding of birth control to this modern rationale has made this so-called sexual freedom work for women. It is an ensnaring, inhibiting kind of freedom which damages the dignity of womankind.

The virtue of chastity is irrevocable. It can never be obsolete simply because it represents not only the commandment of God but also the cumulative wisdom of humanity in its corporate struggle upward from savagery. The nature of the female is to demand a permanent relationship. This is true also of the mature male. It is only the psychologically arrested, adolescent male who wants and demands sex without commitment. He would exploit his companion and rob her of a home and children, the most precious of God's gifts, that he might satisfy his momentary desires. What kind of maturity is that?

So in the light of this, I ask you: Isn't it pathetic that the loss of virginity has become a badge of liberated womanhood, a prestige symbol—so much so that some girls even boast about affairs when they have never had them? Our youth are being bombarded with the nonsense that experimentation before marriage is the only means of testing compatibility. But does not experimentation demand a similar environment? Compatibility cannot be tested by a series of trials in a social vacuum, on the back seat of a car on a dark road, in restraining circumstances where all the moral pressures of a moral universe frown down upon you.

True sexual happiness comes progressively as a part of a relationship which is projected as a permanent commitment in a house where everything is shared in love and faith, where a home is being built and children are planned for and produced. All that you can learn from superficial experimentation is that you are physically attracted to one another, and you know that already.

I wish I could tell you of the many young wives who come to me under unbearable psychological pressures which have followed them for years, because they became pregnant before wedlock. Even those who married soon thereafter are disturbed. I have a strong admiration for the frankness of young people today. They come saying, "If I only had been wise enough to know that marriage should be a supremely precious event in one's life." If it issues only in what has been going on for sometime, its glamor and its spiritual quality may be permanently damaged.

Love and Loyalty

The Apostle names two other virtues of which members of the church must be examples: love and loyalty. No English word can adequately translate this unique Christian love. It is not the affection of a man for a maid, which comes so unbidden to the heart that no one seems to be able to control it. This love is an affair of the will in which a man so subdues his self-centered desires that he is able to care supremely for others. Romantic love is primarily self-centered. We desire a mate because of what she can do for us. Christian love is the ability to care so much for others that nothing they can ever do against us will cause us to cease caring for them. If we have this love, no harm that others may do to us will make us bitter and unforgiving. This is the kind of love which God has for us. It is only when we are in his control that we can have this love for others.

The final virtue which Christians must exemplify before the world is loyalty. This means that we are to have a constant, unwavering commitment to Christ. The true soldier is one who asks no reward save the privilege of fighting for his king. He is like the Spartan of old who was rewarded for a victory in the Olympic games by being permitted to stand beside his king in battle. Plutarch tells of a Spartan wrestler who was offered a bribe to give up the struggle. He would not submit and after a fierce struggle, he won the contest. Someone mocked him saying, "Well, Spartan, what have you gotten out of this costly victory?" His reply was, "I have won the privilege of standing in front of my king in battle!" Loyalty demands of Christ's servants that no matter what light may shine or what shadow may fall, we shall be true to him.

In those days when the world stood amazed at the strange qualities which set the people of Christ apart from all others, the historian, Pliny, wrote to the Emperor Trajan: "They are accustomed to bind themselves by an oath to commit neither theft nor robbery, nor adultery, never to break their word, never to deny a pledge that has been made when summoned to answer for it." When Christianity was launched in this world, the followers of the Nazarene took a pledge to be pure, to maintain an unconquerable good will for others, and to be forever loyal to Christ.

You may say, "Once I took such vows also, but they were broken long ago. What hope have I of knowing that shining purity which seems to belong to another world? What grace is there for me?"

Joseph Fort Newton tells of a woman who came to his study in the London City Temple. "As a girl she must have been very beautiful—English women change so terribly about twenty-five or thirty. She was hesitant and ill at ease, saying that she had attended a few services at the City Temple and wanted to talk with me, provided I would talk with her.

'Somehow I felt that you would listen to me,' she said. 'In spite of the fact that until recently I was a woman of the streets.'

'How did you come to enter such a life?' I asked. 'Of course you need not tell unless you want to—what you say to me is buried in my heart.'

"Then followed a pitiful story of a happy girlhood in a Midland city, how she was married, had a child who died, how her husband was first unfaithful and then went to the war and was killed. 'It was foolish, I know,' she added, 'but I gave up and let go, and when a woman falls, she goes to the bottom.'

'What about your manner of life hurt you most?' I inquired.

'Apart from its sinfulness, I dreaded most the awful loneliness of it—I was an outcast shunned, except by men who had evil passions.'

'Until recently, you said. What arrested you in your way of life? I should be interested to know, if you care to tell me.'

'In Piccadilly, Sir, one evening I saw a woman with a little girl, the most heavenly human being I ever saw, with big blue eyes and a crown of golden curls. The child smiled at me—and my evil life collapsed.'

'And a little child shall lead them,' the Bible tells us. . . ."

"A little child shall lead them" (Isa. 11:6).

Dr. Newton assured her of God's willingness to forgive. She sobbed her way through the Lord's Prayer. Later, a tiny note was placed on his desk saying simply, "You taught me that the love of God has no limit. It saved me. Thank God and you!" [1]

2

Breaking the Spell of Despondency

Isaiah 59:19

> So shall they fear the name of the
> Lord from the west, and his glory
> from the rising of the sun. When
> the enemy shall come in like a
> flood, the Spirit of the Lord shall
> lift up a standard against him.

Dvorak's symphony, *From the New World,* carries
the soul on the majestic march of the "Largo" while the
listener is continually haunted by familiar notes. Soon it
comes through to him that this masterpiece has been woven
out of the familiar music of the Southland, the sublime
spirituals of the Negro people. The music was wrung out of
the anguish of slavery, dipped in the tears of exile, and
baptized in the hope of freedom. Over-arching its anguish
ring the voices of a redeemed people singing their song of
faith. It is ultimately the dynamic symphony of the courageous, victorious soul. Here is music that breaks the spell of
despondency.

Despondency is so much a part of life that almost unconsciously we sing with Stephen Foster, "All de world am sad
and dreary, ebrywhere I roam." The reason we find such
comfort in the Negro spiritual is because he had so much

reason to be sad and his music got him through his sadness. The sadness of our time is all the sadder because it often suffocates the soul when there is no apparent cause for it. Our world is often dark and dreary because we want it that way. We feel if we can only convince ourselves that the world is innately bad and that there is nothing we can do about it, then we are not responsible for doing anything. We thus plunge deliberately into dark, murky melancholia in search of a refuge from responsibility.

Contagious Joy

When we are in such a mood, we place ourselves at the mercy of our circumstances and our companions. And there we remain until God sends someone to lift our spirits. I shall not soon forget the cheerful physician who boarded our plane in Houston and with a ringing voice said, "A pleasant morning, isn't it?" Then the plane settled down when the journey was ended and as he left the plane he turned and said, "A smooth journey, wasn't it?" Unconsciously, he had set the mood for every passenger on board that plane.

When our Lord commanded us to be of good cheer, he undoubtedly did so because he knew that people are not cheered by circumstances or by their own meditation nearly so much as they are by other people who see the beauty of life all about them and share it. When Oscar Hammerstein wrote the lyrics for that marvelous musical, *Oklahoma!*, he drew his inspiration for the opening song from the stage directions for the first scene:

It is a radiant summer morning several years ago, the kind of morning it is which, enveloping the shapes of earth—men, cattle in the meadow, blades of the young corn, streams—makes them seem to exist now for the first time, their images giving off a visible golden emanation that is partly true and partly a trick of imagination, focusing to keep alive a loveliness that may pass away.[1]

Oscar Hammerstein knew that these words were far too lofty to be wasted simply upon stage directions. Therefore, from them he drew the inspiration for that wonderful song, "Oh, What a Beautiful Mornin'!" It is a song that spreads its balm of healing over every listening heart.

A Part of Life

Any normal heart can sing when the day breaks all glorious and golden. Yet, many a morning spreads only a garment of gray over a dark and dismal world. Life is made up of sunshine and shadows. The strong soul must keep his courage when the sun has hidden its face for many days.

Disappointment often throws a cloud over the face of life's sun. So often disappointment diffuses itself across every man's daily life. There must be someone on earth whose dreams have all come true, whose plans have all turned out well; but I have never known such a person.

Almost everyone suffers some disappointment. Here is a young man who felt called of God to be a medical missionary. He worked during the summer and saved what money he could. His mother added to it and he went away to college with high hopes. Warm, new friendships were formed. His world was bright with promise. Then comes the telegram. His father has died of a heart attack. He must go home and help care for the smaller children—no more university for him. All of his dreams are suddenly shattered. Do you marvel that he is very despondent?

Here is a man who labors for half a lifetime in business. His big opportunity breaks. He borrows from family and friends for his grand venture. The company has misrepresented its product. The competition is fiercer than ever. A long, lingering illness of a loved one drains his spirit. Medical bills mount. The burden and the heat of the days are telling on him. The years have taken away his resilience and buoyancy. Financial embarrassment and physical collapse seem imminent.

Here is a young girl who dreamed of marrying her childhood sweetheart. No other thought had ever been hers save that one day she would have her own home and children. Then suddenly, love is withdrawn. Her love leaves town, never to return, and the path before her seems solitary.

Here is a soul created for music. No money has he for lessons. He will be a clerk in a shoe store all his days while his soul shrivels and the music within him dies. Here is another, born to till the soil in God's great, wide, wonderful out-of-doors, who must slave within the walls of an industrial plant.

The more idealistic we are, the more despondent we may become. When you live in a city where public health is made the pawn of politics, where the educating of children is left to the whims of illiterate politicians, where smoke fills the air and debris lies in the streets of what might be one of the loveliest places on earth, where not even the house of God is kept clean and beautiful, how can you keep from being despondent? Those of us who believe in truth, goodness, and beauty and seek to stand for purity and righteousness cannot look upon the pathetic ineptitude of men who fail to see the real needs of our society, and remain unmoved.

The Way Out

How, in a world like this, can we avoid being despondent? We cannot avoid it altogether. Jesus did not avoid it. He was often sad. He was called a man of sorrows, and yet, he did not remain sad. Although his anguish in the garden was so severe that his body broke under the strain and his sweat was as great drops of blood, there still remains that shining sentence which describes his final attitude even toward his cross: "Who for the joy that was set before him endured the cross, despising the shame, and is set down at the right hand of the throne of God" (Heb. 12:2). Our Lord did not intend that we should remain despondent. Here, then, are four ways to help break the spell of despondency.

Take the Long Look

Henry Sloane Coffin, who was for many years president of Union Theological Seminary in New York City, tells of walking with William Howard Taft down the street in Washington one morning. It was shortly before Mr. Taft's death and during those tense days when it seemed that the League of Nations was on the verge of collapse. Mr. Coffin turned to Mr. Taft and asked him what he thought of the future of the League of Nations. William Howard Taft turned and looked full into his face and told him he ought to know enough about this world to know that ours is a world in which the best things always get crucified. But, he added, they rise again.

That is our hope and therein lies the power to break the spell of despondency, the hope that truth crushed to earth will always rise again. It is only through struggle and often through death that better life is born upon this earth.

Cultivate Concern for Others

Again, we can make our despondency less personal if we will cultivate a genuine concern for others. What a marvelous sentence it is in the book of Job which tells us that "the

Lord turned [away] the captivity of Job, when he prayed for his friends" (Job 42:10). Now, if we pray for our friends with the ulterior motive of healing ourselves, there is no power in that kind of prayer to heal us. Such praying is altogether superficial, hypocritical, futile, and empty. Such praying is of no value to ourselves or to God. But to be so genuinely and compassionately concerned for others that we can forget ourselves, that does have an amazing therapeutic power.

For one thing, we come to see that by contrast our lot is not really as grim as we had imagined. John Donne was the greatest dean St. Paul's in London ever had. He was not only one of the greatest poets of English literature, but he was also one of the most practical men who ever stood in the pulpit. One time he preached on such a practical theme as "What to Think About When You Are Sick." In that sermon he told his congregation to be grateful for the fact that they could even die surrounded by loved faces and tender hands. He reminded them that many men breathe out their souls gazing into eyes that are as hard as the flint of the street upon which they lie. Many lie down grotesque in the antics of death without ever a comforting cordial to be placed to their lips. Many die under such conditions without complaint. A woman, who continually complained about her aching limbs, ceased her complaints when she saw a woman who could move neither her hands nor her feet and could not even move her head without pain.

Restoring Your Confidence

We can also break the spell of despondency by asking God to restore our lost confidence in our fellow men. Nothing is more debilitating than the mood of Elijah when he cried, "The children of Israel have forsaken thy covenant, thrown down thine altars, and slain thy prophets with the sword; and I, even I only, am left" (1 Kings 19:10). There is an ancient legend which tells that when Moses pled with God for permission to enter the Land of Promise, God said:

You lost faith in yourself and I forgave that, for this can happen to the best of men. You lost faith in me and I forgave that, for stronger faith may emerge from an honest, temporary lapse of faith. Then you lost faith in people. This I cannot forgive, for you cannot enter the Land of Promise alone.

On the other hand, few things are more bracing than to have strong confidence in the potentiality of redeemed men. When things are dark, look upon men who are as radiant as the face of the morning, through whose blood the streams of God's energy flows, who have faith that comes from heaven, and strong, stalwart courage that comes straight from the heart of God.

That which provoked the Pharisees most about Jesus was that he trusted men, believed in them, believed that every man is capable of mediating the presence of God. His belief in them pulled the best out of them. He was able to stimulate the best in men and through this to drive out the worst. People were sacred in the sight of Jesus, not because they were gods, but because they were God's. They belonged to God. Anything that belongs to God is sacred. Only one power is stronger than man's faith in God and that is God's faith in man.

Look Up

Finally, we can break the spell of despondency by remembering that there are unfailing springs of divine grace that are available to every trusting heart. When God looks out across the world, he does not ask any man in the ranks of the kingdom of God to bear anything alone. On the other hand, he never promises to any one of us that we are going to evade the darkness. He does not say, "I will keep you out of the dark waters." What he says is infinitely better than that: "When you walk through these dark waters I will be with you." "I will never leave thee, nor forsake thee" (Heb. 13:5).

Three centuries ago, in the Tower of London, Lady Jane Grey wrote an immortal letter. In it she said that tomorrow she would place her head upon the block. A young, fresh, English beauty she was, with life and love before her. Yet she possessed something infinitely more precious than that— a grave, noble mind and a pure heart. She wrote to the Protestant leaders of England: "Fight manfully on. The loss of a few men does not mean the loss of the cause. Fight manfully on for the battle is God's and the victory will be ours." She somehow had come to the truth which Isaiah the prophet expressed: "When the enemy shall come in like a flood, the Spirit of the Lord shall lift up a standard against him" (Isa. 59:19).

The greatest man of this century was Winston Churchill. Speaking once before the British Parliament, he said that often he wondered, as he looked out and saw the little children playing at their cheerful games, what would lie before them if God should weary of mankind. In the gospel we have the bedrock assurance that God will never weary of mankind. The great, central cross on Calvary's brow is our assurance. The evil of the earth can never be stronger than it was there. It can never be greater than when those malign forces converged on Calvary to crucify the Lamb of God, whose only sin was in the evil imaginations of the deluded minds of malicious men who would crucify him before they would continue to bear the searching, searing gaze of Christ upon their souls. Evil can never be stronger than it was at Calvary. Yet, even there it could not break the love of God. "Having loved his own . . . , he loved them unto the end" (John 13:1). The silence that is among the starry skies, the sleep that is among the lonely hills is theirs who rest in that love.

3

Living by God's Calendar

Matthew 6:34

*Therefore do not be anxious about
tomorrow, for tomorrow will be
anxious for itself. Let the day's own
trouble be sufficient for the day
(RSV).*

What a strange tyranny time holds over life. We
are not only made by our decisions but also by the timing of
our decisions. There are some decisions which time makes
for us. You may hold a ticket for the most luxurious quarters
on the *Queen Mary,* but if you are not there when she sails,
your sailing on that ship at that time will have been decided.

The timing of your life is vastly important. So often in our
religious thought we think so much about eternity and the
future that we forget that there is a sense in which today is a
part of eternity. We must not empty the living moment of its
value. Eternity does not squander time. Perhaps this is the
reason our Lord said to us that we should live life a day at a
time.

On the shores of Kun Ming Lake in Japan, there stands a
mammoth bronze ox, on the back of which are engraved
these words, written eight hundred years before Jesus was
born:

This little strip of light twixt night and night, let me keep bright today. And let no shadow of tomorrow in sorrow from the dead yesterday gainsay my happiness today. And if tomorrow shall be sad or never come at all, I've had at least today.

One reason we allow our days to be so dark and our nerves to be so drawn beyond all human endurance is because we try to crowd every conceivable problem of the future into today. Through our imaginations we draw all of the burdens of all our tomorrows into a moment of time.

Every boy, be he young or old, loves Robert Louis Stevenson. His *Child's Garden of Verses* made him the poet laureate of the nursery, and his *Treasure Island* will forever live as a masterpiece of romance. He lived in the grips of searing, unrelieved pain from his earliest childhood; throughout life he was tormented. Yet, in the midst of his most bitter days, he taught us how to stay on top of life. He said that any man can get through until nightfall.

A Day at a Time

Jesus knew that life is so hard for many of us that it would be disastrous for anyone to add to the burden of the day the burden we imagine we may carry tomorrow. Therefore, he said, "Take therefore no thought for the morrow: for the morrow shall take thought for the things of itself. Sufficient unto the day is the evil thereof" (Matt. 6:34). Jesus was not saying that tomorrow is unimportant. He was not forbidding wise and careful forethought. Jesus never counseled indifference toward one's responsibilities. He never said, "Quit work and let life take care of itself."

The truth is that Jesus, who trusted most perfectly in God, was a hard toiler. All day long he labored at the carpenter's bench. It is true that he said of the birds of the heavens that

God feeds them, yet even the birds must build their nests and go after the food which God provides.

There is nothing in the above passage to forbid our providing for our security for tomorrow. What Jesus said was, "Sufficient unto the day is the *evil* thereof." What he meant was: do not stagger under tomorrow's evils today.

What Jesus was urging was that we should live by God's calendar, which means living a day at a time. God, who created life, knows the way it can be lived best. The only way life really works is God's way. God separated every day from every night and he made every day a complete compartment of life. The person who tries to violate the laws of God in the natural realm by working late into the night or into the next day is not living, he is dying. How I wish I could persuade everyone of the truth of that before he has the bitter experience of learning it for himself.

When life becomes too crowded and cluttered and it seems that we shall never be able to get our work done, then is the time to remember that promise of God, "As thy days, so shall thy strength be" (Deut. 33:25). The God who appoints our responsibilities will match every responsibility with his strength. Someone has said that the best thing about the future is that God gives it to us a day at a time. Everyone, at the beginning of each new day, should look realistically only at what he has to do that day, and then give himself enthusiastically and ardently to the performing of the task for that day. The hardest work in this world is not as bad as the brooding which leads to pathetic melancholia and self-pity. Work will never wear us down so much as cowardly self-pity. And why should tomorrow be any harder than today? Is not today the tomorrow you worried about yesterday?

Then welcome the challenging hardships of life. The most

heartrending pain is far better than that pampering of the self which leads to constant depression. What inspiration there is in those words of Garibaldi to his soldiers which he had gathered from all over Italy. A heterogeneous, undisciplined crowd of peasants they were, yet Garibaldi's words transformed them.

Soldiers, I offer you danger, struggle, fatigue, and death. The chill of the cold night in the free air, the heat under the blazing sun will be yours. I offer you no lodging, no munitions, no provisions, but forced marches, perilous watches, and continual struggle with bayonets against batteries. Those who love freedom and their country may follow me.

You don't wonder that he never wanted for followers. Jesus Christ never pampered people. He appealed to the strong heroism of the soul when he said, "In the world ye shall have tribulation; but be of good cheer; I have overcome the world" (John 16:33).

Never Alone

We can live a day at a time, for Christ offers to live with us. On the walls of an ancient Scottish castle are engraved these words: "When Jesus comes, the shadows depart." Samuel Rutherford, after a night in a cold, damp prison, said: "Last night, Jesus came into my cell and every stone shone like a ruby." Christians have always felt that. The earliest Christians said of Jesus, "He has turned our midnight into morning."

When we look at him, we see that he never lost time frantically rushing to and fro. He never felt that God required him to work after the energy of his body had been exhausted. There were some disciples in his band who felt that overexertion was necessary, but Jesus said, "Come ye yourselves apart into a desert place, and rest a while" (Mark 6:31).

Longfellow must have had this in mind when he wrote:

What secret trouble stirs thy heart?
Why all this fret and flurry?
Dost thou not know that what is best
In this too restless world is rest
From overwork and hurry? [1]

To live life a day at a time, to fill it full of the goodness of honest toil, to help others to live like that will make tomorrow bright with promise.

No Other Alternative

Finally, you must take life a day at a time simply because it is the only time you really have. This is the only realistic attitude toward life. In fact, the only time you have is this very moment. Every moment is a microcosm of eternity. The only reality in your life is not what you hope to do tomorrow but what you are doing today. Every day we intend to rectify and adjust our lives according to the will of God. This intention only adds to our guilt unless we carry it into action. We are continually putting off into a tomorrow which we do not have, responsibilities which God has given us today.

Soren Kierkegaard has been called the greatest Christian thinker of the last generation. He believed that no man is alive today who simply acts as a spectator toward the ultimate issues of life and death. The only man who knows real existence is the man who, here and now, infinitely and forever, gives himself to the call of Christ.

This existentialism, which is so much in the discussion of Christian thinkers today, emphasizes immediate commitment. Descartes said, "I think, therefore I am." The existentialist would say, "I choose, therefore I am." The essence of our humanity is in our choices, for by our choices we make our personalities. From the standpoint of existentialism, an uncommitted person is no person at all. Suspended judgment is the road to moral suicide. Man must act or he is not a man.

Kierkegaard contended that there are only two kinds of people: the drivers and the drifters. He said that he felt compelled to run after every man in the street and ask him the question: Are you alert or inert? A master or a slave? A creator or a creature? A lifter or a leaner?

Have you ever honestly faced the great fact that every moment is Christ's moment and in every moment Christ is saying something specific to you? He calls us above our moral neutralities. He is no longer patient with us in our moral mediocrity. He reminds us that we are the sons of God. He calls us to forget this meager plan which we have made for ourselves and to commit ourselves to the high challenges of God. He calls us to do something about it in this very moment, to make some supreme, decisive dedication of life which will rid us of all indifference.

This means that living life a day at a time is not a leisurely, relaxed, irresponsible way by which we may drift through the world. It means that we have to put into every moment precisely what God wants in that moment.

Every moment God is confronting his lost creation with this question: What will you do then with Christ? You say, "I will do nothing with him. I will wait." God asks, "What think ye of Christ?" Youth answers, "I am too happy to think." Then youth passes into manhood. Manhood replies, "I am too busy to think, more money and more security first and then I will think." Manhood passes unconsciously into middle life and answers, "I am now afraid to think. I have become the victim of certain pressures from which I can never be released." Then come the declining years and we say, "Now, there is nothing but illness. I am too ill to think. I want only sedation, only escape from life." Then death comes and it is too late to think. Then comes eternity and forever to think.

Four hundred and fifty years ago on Palm Sunday in the city of Florence, the matchless preacher, Savonarola, stood before his congregation and in the midst of his sermon cried out: "It is God's will to give a new head to this city of Florence!" Then there was a long pause followed by a brief suspense in the congregation. Then he declared: "It is God's will to make Christ the King of Florence!"

Christ is seeking to become your king. He is seeking now to become king of your calendar which means you must take him as king of every moment and king of every day. Only thus can he be king of your vast eternity.

4

The Way Out of Worry

Philippians 4:6–7

Be careful for nothing; but in every thing by prayer and supplication with thanksgiving let your requests be made known unto God. And the peace of God, which passeth all understanding, shall keep your hearts and minds through Christ Jesus.

All normal people worry and this may be good, for the freer some people are from anxiety, the more worthless they are. We worry because we are human. As human beings there are three things about us that make us worry: we are dependent and, therefore, insecure; we are spiritual and, therefore, never fully at home in a purely physical environment; we are moral and, therefore, never at ease when we are doing wrong.

So many things threaten our existence and thwart our pleasure. Because we are spiritual beings we are often bored. Boredom is the forerunner of worry. Still, boredom may be a blessed reminder that we were not made for dull preoccupation with physical things. Because we are made in the image of God, obsession with the physical and material side of life soon becomes intolerable to us. The soul seeks to break out of this stifling prisonhouse to soar in the spacious realm of the spirit; for when the spiritual nature of a man is suppressed, great anxiety sets in.

Not only are we spiritual beings, we are also moral beings. Therefore, when we do wrong, we are haunted by a sense of guilt. Because guilt threatens our good opinion of ourselves, it turns into self-condemnation. Then we begin to fear that others will uncover our sins. We cannot bear the thought that others should censure us. Our sense of well-being is too much bound up with the approval of others. More than that, whether we will admit it or not, we fear the disfavor of God.

Separation Causes Anxiety

The gravity of our offense does not greatly matter. We become anxious about it because anything that threatens our relations with others and with God threatens our very existence. Our existence is bound up with the approval of our friends and of society at large and, above all, with the approval of God. The thought that we have rebelled against the God in whom "we live, and move, and have our being" (Acts 17:28) and the knowledge that separation from God means the thwarting of the very purpose for which we were created, plunges us into grievous anxiety.

The person who flaunts his defiance in the face of all moral law, is dishonest in his dealings, drinks excessively, and breaks his marriage vows, often does so because he is in search of a refuge from anxiety. This kind of self-expression brings frustration instead of fulfilment, because it turns the reins of life over to the lower side of our nature until we are dominated by evil. Self-expression is good only when it is the higher self which is being expressed. This kind of expression is possible only through the discipline of our animal nature. What fearful conflict rages in the soul when our animal nature overpowers those finer aspirations for which God created us! This conflict creates dreadful anxiety. The mind becomes overanxious and accelerated until, however tired the body may be, sleep will not come to put the soul to rest.

Solving the Problem

You say, "But many of these anxieties come because of my past. I can do nothing about them." Some of this is true, yet, it ought to encourage us to know that there is a trend among modern psychologists toward placing more emphasis on our present tensions than on our past experiences. This assures us that there is something we can do about our worries. If this were not true, our Lord would never have said that we should not be anxious. Let me then picture a seven-step stairway by which you may climb out of your chronic worry:

1. When you stand on the first step you must face your worries frankly and see exactly what they are. You must refuse to camouflage them. When you camouflage your worries they do not go away. They simply scatter and multiply. If you are worried about somebody's opinion of you, or about the possibility of having cancer, or the likelihood of losing your job, or the fact that you have no security for old age, it is far better that you face the worry realistically than that you should allow your distress to spread until you are worrying about everything that could conceivably befall you.

2. The first step of the stairway then is labeled with your specific worry. The second step is labeled "decisive action." You say, "I am worried about cancer. What can I do about this?" It will do no good to toss through the night thinking of

how many of your family and friends have died with it. You should see a doctor. There is no particular heroism in saying, "I will spare my family and friends. I will bear this alone." By such egocentricity you soon become morbid and make yourself unbearable even to those who are closest to you. You must summon your courage and cast out your fear by facing the truth about your condition.

3. The third step has a sign of caution on it. Here it is: Never make a major decision when you are tired, depressed, or hungry. You may easily panic after a long battle with influenza or after waiting at the bedside of a sick child or after a long season when the weather has been unfavorable and the sun has refused to shine. Delay major decisions until a better day.

4. Remember as you climb the fourth step of the stairway that the worst you fear will probably never happen. Such a sentiment has been expressed in this poem:

> Tomorrow's bridge, as I look ahead,
> Is a rickety thing to view;
> Its piers are crumbled, its rails are down;
> Its floors would let me through.
>
> The chasm it spans is dark and deep
> And its waters foam and fret—
> I have crossed that bridge a thousand times
> Though I never have reached it yet.
>
> It has crashed about me and let me through
> Although it is miles away;
> But strange, the bridges I have crossed
> Have all been safe today.
>
> Perhaps I shall find, when I reach the one
> That lies in the distant blue
> Some hand will have mended its rickety floor,
> And its piers will be strong and new.

> And I shall cross over, light-hearted and free
> As a bird on the buoyant air;
> Forgive me, O God, for my fearful heart,
> My anxious and foolish care.[1]

5. Another step on this stairway out of worry is to work at breaking the monotony of life. Compel yourself to find some recreation. Get your mind off your worry by reading a good book or going to the theater or taking a long walk or by playing golf. The mind must have laughter and relaxation or it will break.

6. Then, above all, have a healthy religion and work at it. This includes putting the horizons of heaven around your life. It includes keeping the gates of prayer open to the throne of God's grace. It includes liberal giving to share the gospel and to help others. For one thing, when you give to others it strengthens your faith in the liberality of others and buttresses you against the day when you might be in need. It includes obeying the supreme command of the Saviour by regarding the proper priorities of life. "Seek ye first the kingdom of God, and his righteousness; and all these things shall be added unto you" (Matt. 6:33).

But you say, "Are not religious people as prone to worry as others? Are they not often more given to anxiety than those who take life as it comes?" It is true that many Christian people are more concerned and compassionate than others. Yet, we must not identify this with chronic anxiety. At the same time, we cannot deny that many profess the Christian faith and remain chronic worriers. Why then has their religion done so little for them?

Often we find such people professing a dull, prosaic orthodoxy which does little more than affirm a belief in the existence of God. They actually have nothing but a pathetic substitute for a real religion. They never have known a personal encounter with the living God. They have no awareness of his presence, no genuine love for him, no vital trust in him. When there is awareness, love, trust, and commitment to the God made known to us in the face of Jesus Christ, the brooding clouds of life are broken up by the bright sunlight of hope.

There is powerful support for the necessity of faith in God in much modern psychiatry. In his *Modern Man in Search of a Soul*, C. G. Jung declared that in the course of his practice, he had found no patient over thirty-five years of age whose breakdown had not been due in the last resort to a lack of religious faith. Moreover, he added that none of them had been really healed who did not regain his religious outlook.

Dr. Stafford-Clark also insists on the necessity of having some system of belief if we are to have and to retain mental health. He assures us that so logical is this need that no one can discard the Christian belief in God without having to substitute for it other beliefs. He adds that the substitutes for a central awareness and acceptance of God are disastrous illusions. If God exists, there is no substitute for him. If he does not, existence itself is without ultimate meaning! This is simply what Jesus declared two thousand years ago. This is not the new psychology or the old. It is the essence of common sense and wisdom practiced by mankind for centuries. You may throw it away if you will but you will throw healthy reason away when you do.

A healthy religion helps us to accept that which cannot be altered. Jesus said, "Which of you by taking thought can add one cubit unto his stature?" (Matt. 6:27). Some things in life cannot be changed while others can. A pastor tells of a lady who came to borrow some books on psychology. He asked why she became interested in the subject. Her reply was that in her earlier years she had been painfully jealous of a younger sister who was admired by everyone for her attractive appearance. She said that she was regarded as quite plain compared with her sister. She had hated herself for years when, one evening, the thought suddenly struck her that if she could not be attractive in her appearance, she could be good and kind. She began to take an interest in the poor and sick and tried to be as understanding as possible. Her pastor told her, "When you are old, I think you will manifest a loveliness far greater than any grace your sister now possesses, for real beauty is a matter of the inner life, and it breaks through and transforms the entire personality as the years go on."

One of our deacons told me of walking into a bank and of borrowing fifty thousand dollars on his signature. He said, "This has been one of the most gratifying experiences of my life." I said to him, "You have a good face and a fine, open countenance which reflects your integrity." A banker who was sitting with us said, "You know, the only thing we can base our security upon is the integrity of people." We must often depend solely upon the face to reflect that integrity. It is said that Lincoln once criticized a man's face. He was reprimanded by one who said that a man is not responsible for his face. Mr. Lincoln replied that any man past fifty is responsible for his face.

A healthy religion gives a man grace to accept what he cannot change and the energy to change what should and can be changed. It also gives him the willingness to repent and to receive forgiveness for all sin and failure. When you have a sense of guilt, it will be accompanied by anxiety and you will never get beyond your anxiety until you have been forgiven. One immediate step you may take is to confess your sin before God, repent, and receive his forgiveness.

7. A healthy religion will lift you to that final step on the stairway out of worry. It will give you a hopeful heart. Psychiatrists are telling us often these days that mental health is dependent upon hope. Christianity shows us a future that has purpose and is, therefore, bright with hope.

Dr. Louis Evans tells of a soldier who lay wounded on a field of hard-fought battle. When the roar of the battle had ceased, he could see in the distance lanterns flickering in the falling twilight as the stretcher-bearers made their way across the field to gather the wounded and take them to the hospitals. He was unable to move; he was unable to speak. He lay watching one lantern as it flickered and grew nearer. Soon a surgeon was bending over him. After his diagnosis he shook his head doubtfully and said, "I believe if this fellow lives until sunrise tomorrow he will get well."

Through the long, cold night the soldier could not be moved. All night long he lay on the ground with these words of hope ringing in his ears: "If I live until sunrise, I shall get well!" He turned his eyes toward the east to watch for the vanishing of the stars and the quivering of the east as the light of day filtered through her fading veil. Then, following the sun, his eyes brightened as he remembered the promise: "If he lives until sunrise, he will get well." He thought of his home, the shady lane, the mossy spring, the wife who shyly slipped her hand into his years ago. "I shall look once more," he said, "into her deep, loving eyes." He thought of his children. "If I live until dawning, I shall feel their kisses upon my parched lips and feel their fingers upon my face."

Then the great Christ of God bent down from the skies and with the hand that was pierced with nails, he touched the ebbing life and held it until the sun rose in all of its splendor. The stars vanished and the day dawned.[2]

We are saved by hope even from our worries.

5

Facing Your Fears

Psalm 130:4

But there is forgiveness with thee,
that thou mayest be feared.

Any religion which offers man complete freedom from fear is fraudulent. Man could neither survive, learn, nor become civilized without fear. Rational fear has been the strong ally of human development. Yet, the ability to control fear is a mark of mental stability, emotional health, and spiritual stamina.

Man is born to fear. In childhood we feared going to bed alone because we had learned in infancy our dependence upon our mothers. We feared anything that separated us from her. We feared going to school and plunging into a strange, new world which separated us from those who had given us security. As we grew older, we came to fear the impossible demands each new day made upon us.

Fear is our constant companion. The mother fears for her children. The father fears for his job. We are not always sick nor are we always sinning, but most of us are constantly afraid of something or somebody.

If our fear has a rational cause it may be healthy. If it is excessive and neurotic it may destroy us. This is why the reduction of our fear is so essential in the treatment of mental and emotional disorders.

Healthy religion should teach us how to fear the right things at the right time. It should also teach us what to do when our fear threatens to plunge us into panic. It must teach us how to find faith in the midst of our fears.

Some Sources of Fear

Many who read these words fear their past, for all have blundered and failed and have been embarrassed by their weaknesses. There are dark alleys in our past down which we do not delight to travel in retrospect. Our past reminds us of our finiteness.

We often fear because the present appalls us. Our expanding universe leaves our education woefully outmoded. The clash between adults and young people comes over the fact that adults know so much that is not so and young people know so much they do not really know.

We behold with our unaided eye five thousand stars. With the assistance of a four-inch lens, we may see over two million stars and with a two-hundred-inch mirror, over a billion stars. Our galaxy is composed of probably one hundred billion stars and there are millions of other galaxies spaced about one million light years apart (one light year is approximately six trillion miles). With such astronomical dimensions before us, do you wonder that ancient man once believed that lunacy was induced by contemplating the heavenly bodies?

Harlow Shapley speculates that there are at least ten million billion planetary sites where life might go on. As his universe grows larger man becomes smaller. He trembles and cries out: "Who is sufficient for these things?" We fear the unknown.

Automation threatens our job. Science has prolonged our span of life, but inflation has destroyed our security, so that while we may not fear disease as once we did, we fear hunger and social embarrassment.

Man trembles before the "overkill" stockpile. One pound of H-bomb stockpile material, the size of a golf ball, packs more explosive power than enough TNT to fill Yankee Stadium. The world's nuclear stockpile in 1960 contained an estimated equivalent of thirty billion tons of TNT—about sixty tons for every human being on earth.

We fear the changing structure of our society. All of this causes the intelligent person to tremble. How then may we face our fears?

Directing Fear Creatively

Healthy religion does not suppress fear. It directs it into creative channels. The psalmist guides us with these words: "But there is forgiveness with thee, that thou mayest be feared" (130:4). The mastery of fear is bound up with the proper attitude toward God and with forgiveness. "How commonplace," you say. Yes, and so is bread commonplace, but it is also very precious to those who are starving.

No carol brings sweeter music to the estranged, fearful soul than the assurance of forgiveness. "God," said the prophet, "delighteth in mercy" (Mic. 7:18). Nowhere do we read that God delighteth in power or that he delighteth in justice. But we do read that he "delighteth in mercy."

This is the heart of the gospel. This is the assuring word that has the power to dispel unfounded fear in those who hear and believe it. If you doubt God's forgiveness, then stand on Calvary once more and look into the wounds of Jesus. Look long at his nail-pierced hands and feet, his thorn-crowned brow. Look straight into his heart where the soldier's spear was thrust, from whence flowed the blood and water for the double cleansing of all who trust him. And remember that if there is no forgiveness, Christ died in vain. If there is no forgiveness, all ministers must be silenced. All of our houses of prayer must be closed for they stand in mockery of God and man if there be no forgiveness of sin.

If many a modern psychologist had been writing this passage, he would have completed it by saying, "There is forgiveness with thee, that men may no longer fear God." But the psalmist wrote, "But there is forgiveness with thee, that thou mayest be feared." "The fear of the Lord is the beginning of wisdom" (Prov. 9:10). The reverential awe before the Almighty is the only antidote for irrational, neurotic fears. We must fear him so much that we fear nothing else beside.

The forgiveness of God creates holy, reverential fear that we may not continue in sin. The person who says, "God will forgive, therefore, let us continue in sin," has never known the forgiveness of God. Forgiveness is predicated on repentance which is the steady fear of God which causes us to turn from anything which would sever us from his fellowship.

Fear of God in the biblical sense is not the dread of God. It is that holy awe which causes us to dread anything that could separate us from him.

The Role of Faith

Fear of God is combined with faith in God. Spurgeon said that repentance is faith's twin brother, born at the same time. No one can repent until he believes he can be pardoned, until he has faith in a pardoning God. He may grieve over his sin and dread its penalty until deep remorse sets in upon his soul, but Spurgeon said that that gentle softening of the soul which makes us hate sin because it is committed against such a good and gracious God is not possible until, first of all, the heart has believed that there is forgiveness with God.

Even neurotic fears are not beyond the reach of God's power to enable us to overcome them through reverence and awe of him. The human beings whom you fear might do you harm, but the God and Father of our Lord Jesus Christ holds you in trust when you rightly fear him. "I will put my fear in their hearts, that they shall not depart from me" (Jer. 32:40). Holy, reverential awe makes us continually aware of God's presence.

A certain Indian tribe once a year observed an ancient custom of sacrificing a daughter of the tribe to the Great River, the Father of Waters, putting her in a canoe and sending her out into the raging current where she was certain to be swept over the roaring falls to her death.

One year, the daughter of the old chief was chosen to be the sacrifice. When the time came for the ceremony, the chief did not appear to preside over the ritual for the daughter he loved. The warriors grumbled at the cowardice of their chief. Nevertheless, they took his daughter down to the water's edge, placed her in the canoe, and shoved her out on the bosom of the water. As she reached the middle of the rapids, they saw in the gathering twilight another canoe setting out from the other shore. In it was the old chief. He rowed to the center of the river, clasped his daughter's canoe, pulled it close to his, took her hand, and went with her over the falls into death.

This is the heart of the gospel, that from the other side of the river God has come to us and made the sacrifice and will come to us again. From the other shore we will feel a hand and faith will replace our fear.

6

Escape from Loneliness

Loneliness is everywhere. Here is a secretary who turns on the radio only that she might hear a human voice bidding her goodnight. Here is a mother who has no adult companion; she is so desperate for amusement that she terrorizes her child with a doll dressed as a devil. Here is a well-educated career woman who draws apart from society because she is ashamed of her small-businessman husband. Here is a psychology professor who cannot understand his wife or win the attention of his children. More shocking still, here is a pastor who unburdens his soul to a priest because he has no close ties among his colleagues or his congregation.

Dr. Paul Tournier, the Swiss physician and author of the widely discussed book *The Meaning of Persons,* in his more recent book, *Escape from Loneliness,* has called loneliness the most prevalent malady of our time. What better proof have we than the above examples that this assertion is not fiction but fact.

Our loneliness is the direct result of our sin. Sin has severed us from our rightful companions—but how? First, by creating a spirit of ruthless competition which we identify with free enterprise and almost deify as a part of Christian democracy. Our competition has led us to use each other as pawns in the race for personal success.

We have isolated ourselves by the false belief that freedom means independence to live our own lives regardless of what happens to others. Such freedom is only negative self-affirmation.

We exclude each other by our possessiveness, grasping after happiness as if it were something we could keep to ourselves, forgetting that by its very nature, it is always a community property which can only be had as it is shared.

We destroy community also by our distorted sense of justice, demanding equality when our real need is for love.

A Need for Fellowship

The only way to put an end to our cravings and conflicts and to heal our loneliness is to come back to the fellowship for which we were created—the fellowship of God. Then we shall see that neither individual nor state nor any social structure can be an end in itself. No life reaches its truest and highest fulfilment until it shares in honest and open relationships with all other men whom God has created. In that sense there can never be a solitary Christian.

Our society is so structured now that the busier life becomes for some of us, the lonelier it becomes for those who are dependent upon us for fellowship. Here is one who is lying ill, waiting for the long day to pass when she will hear the steps of her husband who stood long ago at the altar of God and pledged to care for her in sickness and in health until death should them part. Finally, the husband rushes in and announces a business engagement that will take his evening. He departs and the wife is left in unbearable solitude.

Or, here is a family in the full vigor of life and so involved outside the family circle that they overlook that one who is disposed to be timid and dependent for her social nurture upon the immediate members of the family.

But worst of all, here is a married couple who spend much time together but spiritually they are poles apart. One is a Christian while the other is not. They are destined to be separated until the grace of God unites them in the common family of God.

Accept Loneliness As a Part of Life

There is a kind of loneliness which is inevitable. Every soul on earth is sent in a solitary grandeur into which no one else can intrude. Kipling said that the human soul is a very lonely thing. We are born alone; we die alone; and in the depths of our souls, we live alone.

There are certain things we must do for ourselves. Every man must bear his own burden. Every man must repent for himself, trust Christ for himself, and enter the kingdom of God for himself. This does not mean that he can do these things by himself, but it does mean that no one else can do them for him. Those who are closest and dearest to us cannot do these things for us. Even Jesus came into this world to tread the winepress of the wrath of God the Almighty alone.

He entered into the garden with his disciples. Then he took the inner circle, Peter, James, and John, and journeyed a little further. But, finally, our Lord left them and went into the heart of the garden alone. "It was alone my Saviour prayed." Some prayers ought to be prayed alone, when the soul can be in deepest intimacy with God. Our blessed Lord said, "But thou, when thou prayest, enter into thy closet, and when thou hast shut thy door, pray to thy Father which is in secret; and thy Father which seeth in secret shall reward thee openly" (Matt. 6:6).

Strangely enough, this kind of solitude brings the greatest release from physical loneliness.

"Evening, and morning, and at noon, will I pray, and cry aloud: and he shall hear my voice" (Psalm 55:17). Knowing that he hears, we can never be finally alone.

While every soul must have its quiet hours of healing silence, the true saint is never primarily a recluse. A saint is one who shares the nature of God, and our God is not a recluse. He is at work holding every soul of earth, if not in spiritual life then at least in physical life, "for in him we live, and move, and have our being" (Acts 17:28).

It is unspeakable pathos that man receives every beat of his heart and every breath that he draws from God and still stands rebelling against God in the spiritual side of his life. Man has no choice concerning his physical life. If he lives at all, this part of his nature must be grounded in God. He can never be far from God, for God is ever seeking to bring him back. But he can choose whether he will take his soul out of God's hands and send it to destruction.

Give Yourself to God

We cannot escape God by ignoring him, by seizing the reins and driving off in pursuit of our own desires. God lets us go to the very end of the tether, and sometimes the tether stretches to incredible lengths. But it is never long enough to prevent our being overtaken by him. Go as fast as you will and as far as you will, you will never outdistance God. If you are not overtaken by him in grace, you will most assuredly be overtaken by him in judgment.

Francis Thompson, in one of the great poems of all time, describes the relentless pursuit of God in "The Hound of Heaven." Out of his own deep depravity and sin he learned that he could never run beyond God. His flight was a steady attempt to evade God by night and by day. When he reviewed his life, he saw that the years had been one concerted effort to escape from God. Still, there were areas in his mind where God lingered on. He might put God out of the top of his mind but in the depths of the "labyrinthine ways" he knew that God was still there. When sorrows brought the curtains of mist down over his eyes, Thompson persisted in hiding from God. When brighter days came, he still would not acknowledge God's presence. He climbed the mountains of hope, the depths of gloom, but God was still on his trail.

Escape from loneliness can come only as we cease our flight and surrender to him who alone can control those forces that drive us away from God and our heart's true home. We escape loneliness as we give ourselves to doing our Lord's work in this world. His special presence is promised only to those who obey this command: "Go ye . . . and, lo, I am with you alway" (Matt. 28:19–20). It is only the inactive Christian who sits on the sidelines and watches the soldiers of Christ march by who ever doubts the reality of his presence.

At the close of Franz Werfel's *The Forty Days of Musa Dagh,* we find the story of Bagradian, whose Christian faith led him to defend something more precious than heart or home. He remains on the besieged land after his countrymen are evacuated. Not long after the ships sail away beyond the horizon, he is shot from ambush while standing by his son's grave. In falling, he clings to the wooden cross, taking it slowly with him, and lies in death with his son's cross upon his heart.

It is a moving symbol of the magnificent truth that no man comes to his Christian triumph until he lies with someone's cross upon his heart, and no man who lies with someone else's cross upon his heart is ever alone.

7

What About Faith Healing?

It is to be doubted that you will find in all the Bible a more comprehensive statement of the ministry of Jesus of Nazareth than you find in the twenty-third verse of the fourth chapter of Matthew. We are told: "Jesus went about all Galilee, teaching in their synagogues, and preaching the gospel of the kingdom, and healing all manner of sickness and all manner of disease among the people." As we take up our New Testaments, we are immediately impressed with the remarkable balance between the words of Jesus and the works of Jesus, his counsel and action, his teaching and healing. It seems that the evangelists, the writers of our New Testament, were very careful to maintain that balance.

Jesus, the Miracle Worker

Look for a moment at Jesus, the miracle worker.

"Jesus went about all Galilee . . . healing all manner . . . of diseases." Thirty-six of these miracles are carefully described on the pages of our gospels. This would indicate that from the multitude of miracles which Christ performed, the evangelists chose with deliberation those which they included in their accounts. They were eager to present the complete and comprehensive structure of the kingdom of God which Christ sought to build through his mighty works. At the close of the narrative of John's Gospel, it is said, "Many other signs truly did Jesus in the presence of his disciples, which are not written in this book: But these are written that ye might believe that Jesus is the Christ, the Son of God; and that believing ye might have life through his name" (John 20:30–31).

Jesus came into this world as the Great Physician, the healer of the total person. He reached down into the darkest crevices of the human soul and pulled the horrible truth about ourselves to the surface and still, with boundless mercy, said, "Thy sins be forgiven thee" (Matt. 9:2). Yet, he was not concerned exclusively with the soul. We see him healing twisted minds and maimed bodies, restoring the balance of the physical, mental, and emotional health in men's lives. And not only was Jesus Christ concerned with the individual. We see him reaching out into the total life of human society. In the feeding of the five thousand, we see a community miracle as he attempts to supply the needs of the masses and to feed the hungry multitudes.

Not only did he seek to perform miracles in society but all nature felt the impact of his power. He stilled the storm at sea, not only the raging elements beating upon its bosom, but also the storm within the souls of the sailors. He even reached out beyond the borders of time. In the healing of Lazarus he demonstrated his control over death; he demonstrated his power to bring us into an everlasting relationship with God, to break the bonds of death and the grave and to bring us into an indestructible unity with God the Father. Thus his miraculous power permeated every relationship of life.

Some scholars may discover a man in Galilee who performed no miracles, but if they do, they will have to go further back than the New Testament.

The Problem of Belief

Look first at the problem of disbelief. Here is one who sincerely tells us, "I wish I could believe, but I find it utterly impossible. You surely are not going to ask me to lay aside the gains of science to go back to a primitive, superstitious interpretation of life! You are not going to ask me to believe that these untrained men who followed Jesus and who were eager to believe the unusual, who were always laying hold upon miraculous stories and believing willingly, are adequate guides for us in this age of nuclear fission and space exploration!" Such people say to us, "Of course, we know that Jesus of Nazareth was a man of marvelous psychological power, but you don't expect us to believe any longer that he was a miracle worker!"

You cannot be honest in your reading of the gospel narrative without seeing that Jesus was a miracle worker. Yet if you are honest with yourself, you must confess that in your more thoughtful moments these miracles cause you great concern. You live in an age which does not expect the laying aside of the ordinary ways of God in running his universe. You need a dependable universe. If you are honest, no matter how devout you may be, you must at times confess that these miracles which seem to alter the course of the universe are great problems to you. Faith is not that definition in a stanza of an old hymn, "If you trust and never doubt." It is more like this: "If you trust in spite of doubt," or better still, "If your trust transcends your doubt."

Begin with Faith

How are we going to get at this problem? How are we going to try to answer it? First, let us confess that the problem comes because we have approached the question in the wrong way. The primary question to be asked is, "What do you believe about Jesus?" Unless you begin with your faith in him, not even miracles can produce Christian faith. Christian faith is not the product of some miraculous demonstration. Faith must precede the beholding of miracles.

Even less is faith the product of a knowledge of the created, natural universe. No man of genuine faith need ever to tremble over the prospect that empirical science may come and cut loose all of the moorings of his faith. He need never tremble over the thought that one day some truth may be discovered that will utterly destroy his religious foundations, simply because the man of faith has not based his faith on conclusions he has drawn from his knowledge of the natural order. The knowledge that we have of religion has come from the self-disclosure of God in Christ as he personally encounters us and brings us to know one who stands at the beginning and the ending of the creative process.

So the great question in religion is not, what do we believe about this world, but rather who was Jesus of Nazareth? If we can agree that in Jesus of Nazareth God brought his final, ultimate disclosure of himself and that in him God chose to dwell, then we cease raising the question, Are miracles possible? The only remaining question is, Are these miracles recorded on the pages of the New Testament consistent with what we know about God as revealed in Christ?

The answer comes at once. Everything Jesus did was in perfect harmony with everything he taught about his kingdom of heaven. He came into this disturbed world to lift it back into harmony with God's purposes and to restore the broken outlines of the lost creation. His miracles were for the precise purpose of establishing a better relationship between God and man and between man and man.

Where Are the Miracles Now?

You say, "Suppose we can accept the miracles that occurred in the first-century world. The next great problem is, Why do these miracles occur no longer?" The more immediate answer to that is seen in the words of Jesus. He never agreed to work a miracle unless the attitude of those who stood in his presence was one of faith. It is said, "He did not many mighty works there because of their unbelief" (Matt. 13:58). "According to your faith be it unto you" (9:29). He always offered his power, but he waited for faith before he could make it active.

He came in wondrous compassion to offer all the power of God for the healing of the total personality, but he could not make that power effective until men had the right attitude and were willing to open the gates of their lives to him. Here is part of the answer. Our faith has burned low and miracles do not often occur today, but I want you to look across the scene of our religious world today and take heart, remembering that in some quarters of our world faith is growing strong, and that some happenings can only be understood as miracles.

For many years Dr. Leslie Weatherhead of the London City Temple kept a careful record of his evening services at the Temple, carefully recording the cases for whom his congregation prayed and carefully following the aftermath of their prayers. You will find in the appendix of his massive volume, *Psychology, Religion, and Healing,* case after case of healing that has come about after intercessory prayer.

Do you remember the story of the paralytic, carried by four friends to the Master? He was healed not so much because of his personal faith, but because of the faith of the four who bore him. Oftentimes healing comes, quite apart from the faith of the individual.

What About Faith Healers?

Can we believe in faith healers? What are we to say about the religious hucksters who pitch their tents and prey upon the illiterate, exploiting untrained and superstitious people; and what are we to say about those who practice on nation-wide and sometimes on international television programs?

I am most hesitant to speak at this point, for I personally have no doubt that there are instances in which God has worked manifestly through such people. God must work through all of our inadequacies. Only once did he have a perfect preacher. No intelligent pastor ever stands in the pulpit without realizing that if God works at all, he must work through a very limited medium. His power is often demonstrated most clearly against the backdrop of our human frailty.

But having said that, I want to suggest that most of the faith healers that I know anything about have gone quite beyond the New Testament. For example, some of them suggest that if healing does not come the only reason is because our faith is inadequate. Faith is, therefore, regarded as an automatic means of manipulating the Almighty to do our wills and to minister to our whims. On the contrary, faith in the New Testament is centered in submission to the will of God. It is not an attempt to dictate to God but to listen to God's voice and to energetically follow his purpose.

The Divine Alternative

Furthermore, the New Testament reminds us that God always has an alternative. He doesn't have to heal any one of us. He may do something infinitely better for us. He may do exactly what he did for Paul. Paul was a mighty man of faith. No one doubts that. No one doubts Paul's efficacy in prayer and yet, though Paul asked over and over again, healing never came to his body. He bore his "thorn in the flesh" down to the grave. But God said, "My grace is sufficient for thee" (2 Cor. 12:9).

It is the Christian attitude to look upon pain as a part of the world in which we live. No man can completely avoid pain, but we are taught that we are not left alone in our pain. God is always as near unto us and will remain as near as we let him be. We are taught further that one day God will show us the final, complete pattern which he is weaving through all the pain of Christ and the pain of all his followers, for we remember the words of Paul, "Your life is hid with Christ in God" (Col. 3:3). He also reminds us, "If we suffer, we shall also reign with him" (2 Tim. 2:12). The Master has said, "In the world ye shall have tribulation; but be of good cheer; I have overcome the world" (John 16:33).

Many a faith healer has overlooked the fact that in the miracles of the Master there is a foretaste of the final kingdom of God. In his ministry Jesus was giving something of the outlines of his perfect kingdom. While he taught that the kingdom had come in reality, he taught that it had not come in its fulness. We await a day when we shall come to a kingdom where the perfect will of God will be fulfilled and where the leaves of the trees are for the perpetual healing of the nations (cf. Rev. 22:2).

Without the shedding of tears no man can enter Christ's kingdom. If this is not true, what relevance have those comforting words of the Revelation: "God shall wipe away all tears from their eyes" (7:17)? Only those who have wept with Christ will know the rapture of having their tears wiped away.

8

The Forgiveness of God

Isaiah 1:18

*Come now, and let us reason to-
gether, saith the Lord: though your
sins be as scarlet, they shall be as
white as snow; though they be red
like crimson, they shall be as wool.*

So many of our sermons leave the impression that
God's supreme desire is that all of us should walk this earth
under the shadow of guilt, constantly aware of one truth—
that we are sinners.

We would do well to remember that it is not the ultimate
will of God that we should know we are sinners. It is rather
his will that we should know that we are *forgiven* sinners,
that we should have a bright, cheerful philosophy of faith—
faith in God, faith in ourselves, faith in others, faith in the
essential decency of humanity, faith in our capacity to grow
and to develop and to do the will and work of God in this
world. The person who does not have faith—who is always
suspicious of others, who feels that others are plotting
against him to destroy him—is mentally disturbed.

An Unnecessary Burden

One reason we lack faith in ourselves and in others is
because we carry a burden of guilt. We are always under

this shadow of depression because of guilt. Have you ever looked into the circled weary eyes of a man who for half a lifetime has felt that the normal Christian feeling is for him to be constantly aware of his sin? You can tell him that it is not God's will that he should feel so aware and conscious of sin, but rather that he should feel he is a forgiven man.

Then, suddenly, the light will come into those eyes like the breaking of the dawn upon the grey hills and he is like a man who long has worried about a malignancy, who has felt for many months that he had this malady but feared going to a doctor and, finally, he has summoned enough courage to have a diagnosis. After it was over, the doctor assured him that there was only a minor malady and he would not need surgery—he would get well without it—and the burden was lifted.

A man who knows forgiveness is a man who knows his burden is being lifted and feels the elation and ecstasy of it all. He breaks out into the singing of that rapturous hymn, "Happy day, happy day, When Jesus washed my sins a-way!" We need to proclaim this constantly, not primarily because it gives the feeling of a happy, blissful destiny at the end of this life, but because no man is whole and healthy unless he is assured of God's forgiveness.

It is necessary not only that man should know God has forgiven him and is willing to forgive, but that he should keep the feeling of having been forgiven. Let me suggest three reasons why this feeling is essential: First, one needs the feeling of togetherness which forgiveness brings. Second, sin is a tyrant which always exaggerates the feeling of guilt and tells us that we are worse than we really are. Finally, if we do not have the assurance of forgiveness, the guilt will be repressed into the deeper regions of the soul and become a permanent source of anxiety.

Togetherness

You must have the feeling of forgiveness because you were born with the longing to belong, with the need for togetherness. "God setteth the solitary in families" (Psalm 68:6). Religion is never a private matter. It is a personal matter, but it is far from being private. This is why there is no such thing as a solitary Christian. You could never have heard of Christ if you had always lived alone. All the holy commandments of heaven have behind them the need of man for unity and for fellowship.

When we do those things that embarrass others and cause ourselves to be rejected by others, the feeling of isolation becomes intolerable to us. Life becomes unbearable. Sin builds a barrier between the soul and God and between man and man. The supreme need of the prodigal was for a feeling of belonging. He had pleasure, but it was only a surface thing —no deep, enduring joy. He would never really feel secure until he was back at his father's house, back in the family fellowship.

This feeling of estrangement is the mother of all sorrows. It lay behind Cain's murder of his own brother. If Cain could not be acceptable before God, he could not bear the thought that his brother should be separated from him by being acceptable to God. Therefore, to have fellowship with his brother, he would separate him from God, even as he was separated. So he tried to do so by murdering his brother. Separation makes evil aggressive. Evil men must have companionship, as the action of Joseph's brothers portrayed. If they could not enjoy the same favoritism with their father that Joseph had, they would see to it that he did not continue to enjoy it either. They would sell him into slavery.

This is the great problem—this feeling of estrangement—

this great need of man to feel at home, to belong, to be secure, and no man will ever feel it until he knows that he is acceptable to God. He cannot afford to put down his hostility and his distrust of others until, first of all, he is secure in his fellowship with God. He must be loved if he is to act as a human being, and only God can ever completely love him. When he is finally assured of that love, that strong good will that can never be broken, that fellowship which can never be shattered in time or eternity, then he can afford to have the same good will toward his fellow humanity.

Tyranny of Sin

In the second place, we need to know that we have been forgiven because sin exaggerates our feeling of guilt. Sin always tells us that we are worse than we really are and that we are so bad that there is really no need to try to improve. Sin camps so close to the eye that we cannot see anything else.

David said, "My sin is ever before me" (Psalm 51:3). It was so close to him that he could not see the salvation of God. Of course, there was much that was wrong with David, but there was also much that was right with him; for if that were not true, it never could have been said that he was a man after God's own heart. If you will remember his Oriental environment, that he was an absolute monarch with the absolute right to take the life or the wife of any of his subjects, then what becomes most impressive is not his sin but his repentance.

The pathos of it all is that he delayed his repentance so long and allowed this cloud to hang dark between his soul and the face of God. As no parent wants discipline to drive a child away from him, so the God of heaven does not want the feeling of guilt to drive us from him, but rather to draw us to him. What a parent wants is a change in the child's attitude so that the warm, bright family relationship might be restored, and this is what God wants. Jesus could forgive the sin of Zacchaeus, of Matthew, of Peter, not because he took their sin lightly, but because he knew there was something far more basic in the gospel than the fact of sin. That is the fact of the everlasting mercy and forgiveness of God.

Repressed Guilt Is Poisonous

Finally, we must have the assurance of forgiveness because unconfessed, unforgiven sin is repressed into the subterranean regions of the soul where all of the springs of life are poisoned by it. Nothing is more devastating to the Christian life than the repression of guilt. Repression simply means that the feeling of guilt is so intolerably painful that we seek to get it out of the conscious mind by pressing it down into the subconscious realms of the soul. From there its poison spreads, and what is there to do except to try to find certain antidotes for this poison? What we actually do is to prescribe inadequate antidotes for the poison.

Self-righteousness

One is the antidote of self-righteousness. We refuse to admit our guilt. This is the reason the self-righteous person is always so unbearable. The self-righteous person may be compensating for his repressed guilt. Real goodness is never self-conscious. The Holy Joe in the ministry behaves as he does because he cannot afford to be normal. He is afraid somebody will find him out.

Hostility

The second inadequate antidote for guilt which we prescribe for ourselves is hostility toward others. Those who are superior, those whose very goodness sits in judgment upon us and shames us, call forth our resentment and hostility. We are equally hostile toward those who are like us because we see ourselves reflected in them. We do not like ourselves when we are repressing guilt and we do not like anyone that reminds us of ourselves. The reason a trollop utterly hates a trollop is because she hates herself. She cannot like anybody who reminds her of herself.

We strike out even against those who are closest to us when there is repressed guilt in the soul. It destroys the warmest relationships in the family so that no one in the family can relax. Here is a man who has squandered his money upon which his wife has been totally dependent for the financing of the household. She asks him about his salary. His response is abnormal. His temper flares. He says, "I don't have to account to you or anybody else for how I spend my money. It's mine. I made it, and I'll use it as I very well please!" If he had been rational, he would have had to admit that if his wife were a normal housewife, she would have worked an eighty-hour week, probably twice as much as he had. She would have done far more to earn that money than he. But the point is, if he really believed that he had the right to spend his money as he wanted, he did not have to be so overwrought. This kind of hostility is the result of repressed guilt and causes us always to be on the defensive.

Self-built Barriers

If we are ever to overcome this hostility and feel forgiven, we must remember that God did not build these barriers between us and him. We built them. God did not forsake us. We forsook him and we do not have to plead for him to return. If we desire him, he is already present in our desire.

We do not have to explain to God. God understands far more than we about ourselves. Like Christian in *The Pilgrim's Progress,* we must bring our big bag of sins and failures and put them down before the cross and say, "I cannot bear this crushing burden any longer. I do not understand theology. I do not understand psychology and there are many of the teachings of Jesus that utterly bewilder me. But I love him and would like to be like him and would like to follow him."

I cannot guarantee that anyone who does that will be immediately made over. Perhaps he will, but it does not always happen, and I do not see it happen often. The consequences of sin and guilt do not vanish very readily, but one thing will be different. The haunting fear of harsh retribution and that cold, clutching terror over an impersonal nemesis, which so long has dogged your trail, will vanish. You will see that the way of Christ is a friendly discipline with the love of God behind it and the restoration of the soul before it.

Even the consequences of sin were not intended of God to be heartless punishment nearly so much as a way by which a man can come into a restored fellowship with God. When we see this, we can say with Pilgrim:

So I saw in my dream, that just as Christian came up with the cross, his burden loosed from off his shoulders, and fell from off his back, and began to tumble, and so continued to do till it came to the mouth of the sepulchre, where it fell in, and I saw it no more. Then was Christian glad and lightsome, and said with a merry heart, "He hath given me rest by His sorrow, and life by His death." [1]

"I saw it [sin] no more," said Christian. Why not trust God to do that for you?

"Well," you say, "where does repentance come in?" May I suggest again that too much of our evangelistic preaching has been on the negative aspect of repentance. Repentance is not primarily turning away from sin. That could be nothing but the most futile kind of moralism. Repentance is primarily turning to God. Of course, they occur simultaneously, but the basic emphasis is upon turning to God. You cannot rid yourself of your sin. You cannot repent of your sin alone. If you could, Christ, the Lord of Glory, need never have come into this world. If man could repent by himself, a just God could hold him responsible for nothing more. But because we cannot repent for ourselves, here stands the Man of Nazareth clothing himself with all of our frailty, offering to enter into our sin, to repent for us, to enable us to repent, to clothe us with his righteousness until we see what sin is all about and come to have his attitude toward it. Only thus can the power of sin ever be broken.

Forgiving Others

The assurance of our forgiveness lies in our forgiveness of others. If you hold anything in your heart against another, do you wonder that you doubt that God could forgive? It is your refusal to forgive another person his sins that causes you to doubt the ability of God to forgive.

Years ago in a western community a husband and wife were having marital trouble. Their tensions strengthened. The chasm between them broadened. They became so irritable that they could no longer live in the same house. The husband left his business, moved to another town and set up business anew. Years passed. He went back to the city where his wife still resided. He went out to the cemetery where his only son was buried. As he looked down upon the grave, his heart was wrapped in tender memories of his boy.

He heard footsteps behind him. He turned and saw his wife. Their first impulse, of course, was to turn away from one another. Then they realized that they had a common interest in that grave. There, over the dust of their son, they clasped hands, and there was healing.

That is the meaning of the cross. At least, it is a part of the meaning. The God who in Christ identified himself with us in all our shame and sin and sorrow still brings to us the assuring words of the prophet, "Come now, and let us reason together, saith the Lord: though your sins be as scarlet, they shall be as white as snow; though they be red like crimson, they shall be as wool."

9

A Christian Attitude Toward Your Body

Romans 12:1

*I beseech you therefore, brethren,
by the mercies of God, that ye
present your bodies a living sacrifice, holy, acceptable unto God,
which is your reasonable service.*

Marshal Henri Turenné of France was a valiant
warrior who sacrificed greatly that he might bear his witness
for Christ. As he was shaving one morning before a great
battle, his hand trembled uncontrollably until he turned
upon his body and said, "Tremblest thou, vile carcass? Thou
wouldst tremble more if thou knewest where I am going to
take thee this day!" Despite his fear he went on into battle.
There was much that was commendable in his courage
which refused to pamper his body, yet, to call his body vile
was far too derogatory. Weak as his flesh was he could not
have gone into battle without it.

Only once do the Scriptures call the human body vile.
Paul said of Jesus Christ, "Who shall change our vile body,
that it may be fashioned like unto his glorious body" (Phil.
3:21). Paul is comparing the body of flesh with the body we
shall have in eternity. Only in contrast with the body we are
to have in heaven can these earthly bodies be in anywise

58

called vile. The body was created by God and, therefore, could not of itself be evil or shameful. What we do with our bodies may be evil or shameful, but the body as God made it is the crowning glory of God's physical creation.

The fact that Jesus walked this earth in a human body is the final proof that human flesh is not inherently evil. So precious is the body to the men of the Bible that they could never agree with the Greeks, who regarded it as the prison-house of the soul. They preferred rather to believe that the body would, by the grace and power of God, break the bonds of the grave and in the resurrection be transformed into a body suitable for fellowship with God.

Therefore, the reverent person stands in absolute wonder and amazement before his body. The head houses the mind, which is grounded in the mind of God and discerns the ways of God. The eyes are the windows of the soul, letting the boundless beauty of earth and sky shine through. The lips, when inspired of God, are capable of speaking the word of God to uplift humanity and enrich all who hear. The hands are capable of lifting heavy loads, of binding up wounds, and of printing the Holy Scriptures. The feet are capable of running the errands of God and the shoulders have been made broad to bear the heavy burdens of life's day.

Sustained by Christ

Not only were these bodies created by Christ; they are also sustained by him. "In him we live, and move, and have our being" (Acts 17:28). That means that you cannot think one thought apart from the enabling power of Christ, for Christ is the bond which unites knowing minds with a knowable universe. Sin is called moral insanity because it leads to a reprobate mind which rebels against God until it is no longer grounded in the intelligence of God.

The human body is not sustained solely by physical energy. We do not live simply because we continue to eat. Our fathers ate and they are in their graves. "Man shall not live by bread alone, but by every word that proceedeth out of the mouth of God" (Matt. 4:4). Our lives are grounded in his guidance. Should he withdraw his hand, not only would our reason go from us, but the strongest heart would cease to beat despite all the physicians could do.

Christ not only creates and sustains, he also lays the heaviest obligations upon these bodies by redeeming us. "Ye are not your own," said Paul, "for ye are bought with a price: therefore glorify God in your body, and in your spirit, which are God's" (1 Cor. 6:19–20). His thorn-crowned brow purchased our heads that we might "let this mind be in you, which was also in Christ Jesus" (Phil. 2:5). His nail-pierced hands now hold your hands in a vise. The spear which passed through his side now pierces your side and pins you to his heart forever. His wounded feet have bound your feet to run his errands. His death-silenced lips have liberated your lips to proclaim his gospel, and the last drop of blood which flowed from his heart has purchased the last ounce of your energy to do his work in this world. "Ye are not your own, for ye are bought with a price: therefore glorify God in your body, and in your spirit, which are God's."

Solemnly are we warned against dissipating the strength of these bodies. "Ye are the temple of God, . . . the Spirit of God dwelleth in you. If any man defile the temple of God, him shall God destroy; for the temple of God is holy, which temple ye are" (1 Cor. 3:16–17). Just as no tenant has a right deliberately to abuse the house that he rents, which is not his own, even so you have no right to take the ax of dissipation and by violating the known laws of health, batter this temple which belongs to God and in which his Holy

Spirit must dwell if ever you are to be delivered to his everlasting kingdom.

Peter said, "Add . . . to knowledge temperance" (2 Pet. 1:5–6). Sometime ago, Dr. Kenneth MacFarland, educational consultant for General Motors Corporation, spoke to a group of executives and sales people in our city. Referring to the Davidson report on why factory workers are fired from their jobs, he said, "Next to laziness is intemperance." He appealed to those assembled to leave heavy drinking alone. "Strong drink is raging: and whosoever is deceived thereby is not wise" (Prov. 20:1). It isn't very heroic of us to shatter our nervous systems by intemperance and then call upon the Almighty whose laws we have deliberately violated to heal us. What God and humanity need from us is a clear mind, poised nerves, and a steady hand.

Freedom Versus Control

When Paul said, "I keep under my body, and bring it into subjection" (1 Cor. 9:27), he was depicting the constant warfare between the desire for total freedom and the Christian principle of self-denial. "But," we say, "self-expression is a part of our freedom. These impulses and appetites are given us of God!" Indeed they are, but they were given for a divine purpose, not that the purpose of God might be thwarted.

The Christian ideal is not self-expression but self-control. The sex drive is given us as a means through which we may enter with God into the very process of creation. Through this act new life is born and two personalities are fused into one until that new life has a solid fortress of love built around it. Thus the child feels from the beginning that he has been loved into this world through the love of God made real by his parents.

God has given us the soil of this good earth. In its place it is fruitful. We couldn't know life as we have it upon this earth apart from soil in its proper place. But soil out of its place becomes dirt. We do not want it smeared on the faces of our children or tracked across the carpets of our living rooms.

Sex is like the soil which is beautiful in its place yet degrading out of its place. Within the family relationship it is blessed and fruitful sod, but outside of that relationship it is defiling dirt.

A vacuum cleaner salesman deliberately transgressed the commandment of God and violated his marriage vows. When his wife discovered that he was maintaining a paramour in an apartment close by, he admitted it and chided her for not discovering it sooner. In an insane rage she shot her husband's paramour. On the witness stand, though he was not compelled by law to testify against his wife, he deliberately sought through his testimony to secure her execution. The jury acquitted her, but she was doomed to walk through life haunted by her horrible misdeed.

If you say, "How unjust! The man got off scot free!" then look further. Throughout his sales territory the word of his crime traveled. No housewife would open the door to him. The sales manager's telephone was rung continually by irate housewives. Each would say, "You come and get this machine." "Why?" asked the manager. "Isn't it satisfactory?" "Yes," was the reply, "it works perfectly, but I don't want anything in my home that that man's hands have touched!"

The Body and the Personality

Immorality does not work! This drive which God has given us adds to human blessedness only when it is kept within the bounds of the family. The family relationship not only makes possible the creation of a human organism but it also makes possible the development of a human personality. Without the love and security which a family can afford, a child cannot develop into a mature personality. Therefore, when men and women play fast and loose with the physical processes of life, they are guilty not only of the most terrible transgression against God but also the most heinous crime against humanity. They bring life into the world under circumstances which hinder the child's developing a whole personality.

In the Christian religion the body is dear because it is a permanent part of the personality. The New Testament teaches some kind of continuity between our present body and the glorified body beyond the resurrection. Paradoxically, Christianity is both the most spiritual and the most physical of all religions. It binds the body and soul together eternally in the doctrine of the resurrection.

The father of our country, George Washington, had no children of his own. But he loved children most tenderly and cared for several adopted children. His favorite was the little girl whom he called "my Pat." When she was ill, he always held her on his lap. He once said that no laughter ever rang out on Mount Vernon like the laughter of "my Pat." When she was eighteen years of age, he stood at the bedside and held her hand while she slipped into that sleep that knows no earthly waking. Her death threw a cloud of gloom over that great plantation. Washington was never the same after that, for he never forgot the laughter and the physical body of his little girl.

These bodies of our loved ones are intertwined with our hearts. Christian hope has no meaning for us if it does not include the reunion with the beloved. Stephen, the first Christian martyr, in his dying moment saw the Christ on the right hand of the Majesty on High, not as a shining, celestial light, but as the Son of Man. What else could he say except, "Lord Jesus [Man of Nazareth], receive my Spirit" (Acts 7:59)? What else could Browning make David say in "Saul" than this:

> Oh, Saul, it shall be
> a Face like my face that receives thee;
> A Man like to me
> thou shalt love and be loved by forever;
> A Hand like this hand
> shall throw open the gates of new life to thee! [1]

Hear then the word of the Apostle: "I beseech you therefore brethren, by the mercies of God, that ye present your bodies a living sacrifice, holy, acceptable unto God, which is your reasonable service."

10

How to Find the Guidance of God

Genesis 24:27

*And he said, Blessed be the Lord
God of my master Abraham, who
hath not left destitute my master
of his mercy and his truth: I being
in the way, the Lord led me to the
house of my master's brethren.*

David, the great psalmist, speaking of God, said, "Thou shalt guide me with thy counsel, and afterward receive me to glory" (Psalm 73:24). But modern man declares that we must trust entirely in the intellect for guidance and not give way to our whims, which we call religious impressions.

Many things make it hard for modern man to believe in the guidance of God. The study of the stars makes it hard. When the astronomer turns away from his telescope to tell us that the nearest star to the earth is probably twenty-five billions of miles away and that the total number of stars in the universe is something like the total number of grains of sand on all the seashores of the world, our minds are paralyzed by such inconceivable figures and the channels of prayer seem frozen in a universe so vast.

When the geologist, reading the history of the rocks,

estimates the age of our world at some two thousand millions of years, the threescore years and ten of our human lives are less than the twinkling of a star and it seems impossible to assert that such short-lived creatures can hold fellowship with the vast mathematical mind which lies behind the universe. In the bewildering vastness of space and peering down the long vistas of time, it seems so pitifully naïve to ask, "Does God care for me? Is he interested in my activities? Will he guide me in all the details of my little life?" Many give the bleak answer that we must not flatter ourselves by such wishful thinking.

Yet, there are multitudes who stand spanning many centuries in their experience, saying, "God has been near and real and has spoken to my heart." God has not taught us to measure the greatness of things by their vastness. A baby is more than a mountain, for a baby can love. A man is more than a star, for a man can think. Longevity is not the standard of greatness. A man is more than a tortoise even though it be true that the tortoise is the Methuselah of the animal kingdom. Astronomy and geology may conspire to prove the utter insignificance of man, but it is man who is the astronomer and the geologist and something vastly more, he is the child of God. Christ our Lord taught us that God guides his children and that we find our highest fulfilment as we walk in his counsel.

Being in the Way

Let us look at the ancient story in Genesis 24:27 as we seek to know how to find the guidance of God. Here are the words of Abraham's servant as he went in search of a wife for Isaac: "I being in the way, the Lord led me."

Isaac was the child of Abraham's old age, the child of his faith. You remember how God directed Abraham to sacrifice

Isaac on the altar on Mount Moriah, how his hand was stayed by the hand of heaven, how he learned that that which is laid on God's altar can never be lost.

Now Isaac has reached young manhood. It is the fear of his father that he may lose his heart to one of the pagan maidens among whom he dwells. Therefore, Abraham calls his elder servant to him and tells him to go back to Abraham's homeland to choose a wife for his son. Isaac has nothing to say.

I think I know what you young people are saying: "How utterly heartless! It's bad enough to have a parent choose a mate for a child. Who could imagine marrying one whom a hired servant would choose? Does this not utterly destroy that warm, glad adventure of romance which is a part of all true love? Doesn't it destroy the miracle the poet referred to?"

> Two shall be born a whole, wide world apart
> And one day out of darkness they shall stand
> And read life's meaning in each other's eyes.[1]

But look a bit more deeply and you will see that there was far more in the background of this story than the cold-hearted, calculating choice of a hired servant. Eastern marital customs have always been different from our own. The eastern parent lives much more closely to the child. They would tell us, "We know our children and love them very deeply. We know them better than they know themselves. We would not want them to marry one whom they could not love. We, therefore, assist them in finding one whom they can truly love forever." They would remind us that there are fewer divorces in Eastern countries where parents do not permit so serious a thing as marriage to be left entirely to the lighthearted choice of youth. You may be fully assured that Abraham had thoroughly instructed his servant about how to choose a wife for his son.

But, be that as it may, we are soon to know in this story that it was not Abraham's choice nor his servant's but God's choice. Listen again to the servant's words: "I being in the way, the Lord led me."

How God Leads

Notice how God led him. When the servant arrived at the well in the city of Nâhor in Mesopotamia, it was eventide. He made his camels to kneel down. Then he knelt in prayer for God's guidance in choosing a maiden who would come to the well. As he prayed, he came to know how to choose, for he thought, If she offers me water to drink, I shall know that she is kind and compassionate. If she goes further and offers my camels water, I shall know that she is observant of the needs of others and merciful to animals. This was not his own cold reasoning but an impression shaped in his mind by God.

When he had prayed, he lifted his eyes, and behold, there came in the cool of the evening a lovely maiden, Rebecca, with all the grace of an Eastern woman. She was fair to look upon. God, who made physical beauty and who knows the joy it brings to the human heart, intends that it shall have its part in romance. Moreover, she was upright in moral character. She had guarded well those fine and final sanctities which are the crowning glory of womanhood.

The servant of Abraham knew at once that God had guided him to the one who would be forever closest to the heart of Isaac, the son of his master. He, therefore, bowed down his head and worshiped the Lord. "Blessed be the Lord God of my master Abraham, who hath not left destitute my master of his mercy and his truth: I being in the way, the Lord led me to the house of my master's brethren."

The conclusion of this story is in the wondrous statement that when Isaac first saw Rebecca, he loved her and she became his wife. This is the only kind of love that will endure—the love that has the guidance of God and the undergirding of heaven. Nothing can ever destroy such love.

Continuous Awareness

God's love will guide us into perfect human love if we will follow him. But, some are saying, divine guidance seems vague, even unreal; perhaps it is only projected fancy. The reason for this is that they treat God as though he exists only for the emergencies of life. If you want God in the crisis, you must have him in the continuum.

Abraham's servant was a man of continuous prayer. He was commissioned in prayer. As he crossed the burning desert, he prayed to God whom he knew in the continuum. The listening side of prayer must be studied. It is not learned in books but in the quiet hour behind the closed door. There we come to know that it is possible to live under the pressure of God's guiding hand.

The scoffer says, "No, I don't go to church! It is made up of senile old ladies and little children singing, 'Gentle Jesus, Meek and Mild.' When you go to church, you have to leave your intelligence in the vestibule." And the same man will flip a coin and say, "If it comes down heads, I'll do this, or if it is tails, I will do the opposite." But let any scoffer discipline himself in the listening side of prayer and he will know the reality of the guidance of God.

Have you ever been present when a great surgeon diagnosed a case? Here is a man who comes modestly into the doctor's office. He is embarrassed by his condition and a little bit fearful. He lies upon the table and the surgeon bends over him to listen to his heart. The surgeon concentrates. He recognizes the ailment and tentatively diagnoses it. A few days later, on the operating table, his diagnosis is confirmed. How could he know? Not by a few spasmodic listenings a year but by long years of disciplined listening. So the ear that listens to God can hear him clearly.

I heard Dr. W. E. Sangster tell of visiting a widow whose husband had been gone twelve years. Said Dr. Sangster, "He was a good man and left his wife many happy memories, but nothing more." She said, "When my husband went away, I knelt down and put God on his honor and said, 'O God, you have promised to be a husband to the widows.'" Said Dr. Sangster, "Has he been a good husband?" She answered, "You will forgive the quaint expression, but sometimes he comes so near to me that I can feel his hand upon my back." She had cultivated his presence in the continuum and found that he did not forsake her in her crisis.

The classic scriptural example of spiritual discipline is Job. There came a day when his sons and daughters were eating and drinking in the eldest brother's house and the Sabeans fell upon them, took them away, and slew the servants with a sword. The fire fell from heaven and burned up his sheep. The Chaldeans fell upon his camels and carried them away. A great wind blew down the eldest son's house, destroying the young men. What did Job do? He did exactly what he had done every other day. His spiritual discipline carried him through. He fell on his face in prayer and said, "Naked came I out of my mother's womb, and naked shall I return thither: the Lord gave, and the Lord hath taken away; blessed be the name of the Lord" (Job 1:21).

You will always be safe in the crisis if you have known God in the continuum. His guidance will be real to you and nothing will be more precious to you in all your pilgrim journey.

11

How to Get Along with Difficult People

Matthew 5:44

*But I say unto you, Love your
enemies, bless them that curse you,
do good to them that hate you, and
pray for them which despitefully
use you, and persecute you.*

Sometime ago I was asked to speak to the Presidents' Club of the University of Tennessee on the subject, "How to Get Along with Difficult People." This club was composed of more than one hundred presidents of all the student organizations—young people who had already demonstrated qualities of leadership and who were soon to move out into a world of larger responsibility.

There is a passage in the Bible, Matthew 5:38–48, which lists three specific ways in which we may get along with the most difficult people. First, we must accept people as they are; second, we must bear with the limitations of others; and, third, we must learn to control resentment.

Now, this doesn't tell us how we can get along with all people. The greatest person who ever lived on this planet was Jesus of Nazareth. If we are honest, we will have to confess that he didn't get along with all people. Perhaps we have made too much of the gentle Jesus, meek and mild. We have overdrawn the picture of the peaceful, tranquil soul who moved smoothly and peacefully through all the earthly scene. It would be far more true to say that there was scarcely a day in our Lord's life which did not find him in conflict. He said, "I came not to send peace, but a sword" (Matt. 10:34). He couldn't get along with all people. If he had gotten along with all men, it is quite obvious that he would not have been crucified when he was only thirty-three years of age.

There are psychopathic personalities all about us, even among our most immediate companions, with whom we can scarcely hope to get along. If we are honest, we will not upbraid ourselves because of our failure to get along with all men. Yet, looking deeply into the life of our Lord, we find him getting along with many most difficult people. In fact, he seems to have chosen some of the most difficult people to be closest to him. He was quite willing to accept them just as they were.

Acceptance

Accept people as they are. That is my first suggestion. If you would get along with difficult people, you must begin by accepting them just as they are. Jesus of Nazareth, with all of his spiritual power, never sought to manipulate men. He never sought to coerce them nor was he ever so frantic that he sought to drive men. He invited into his intimate fellowship men like the sons of thunder, James and John. These men had such seething resentment in their souls that they could not stand outside the gates of the inhospitable Samaritan village without wanting to strike back. They turned to their Lord with an altogether unworthy request: "Lord, wilt thou that we command fire to come down from heaven, and consume them . . . ?" (Luke 9:54).

There was Peter, one of the most impetuous of all the personalities of the Bible, who could not sheath his sword when one soldier laid bold and ruthless hands upon his Master. He would even sever the ear from the head of the servant of the High Priest. There was no gentleness in him and he had little control over his temper.

Think of the other side. Can you imagine more phlegmatic men than those who gathered around our Lord in the garden —men who were so apathetic and indifferent that they could even sleep in the midst of the greatest crisis Jesus ever knew? It is doubtful that you can ever find in the Scriptures a clearer picture of the true humanity of Jesus than you have in the episode in dark Gethsemane. He knew that tomorrow he would die. He knew that his death would not be an easy one, with his head upon a comfortable pillow, surrounded by loved faces and friendly, gentle voices, by loving hands and tender hearts. He knew that it would not be like that! He would lay down his life on the hard wood of the cross amidst the jeers of the Roman soldiers and the malefactors about him.

Therefore, he went into that garden to pray to God that his high courage might not fail and that his faith would hold him steadfast through his responsibility. After he prayed so earnestly that the very composition of his body began to break under the strain, he came back and found those who were closest to him, whom he had fully expected to bear with him in the moments of his greatest anguish, sound asleep. You don't wonder that he blazed out pointedly at them, "What, could ye not watch with me one hour?" (Matt. 26:40). Isn't that the temptation that often comes to religious leaders? We prepare carefully and painfully as well as time permits. We come to the house of God eager to impart a message and the people do not come; and there is the thought in the pastor's heart, "What, could ye not bear with me one hour?"

Jesus went a second time to pray and a second time he came back. If his prayer had any effect at all upon his disciples, it was not evident, for they were still asleep. When he went away the third time, his prayer was probably changed. His thoughts were turned away from them and he thought of himself primarily, and when he returned still nothing had happened in the lives of his own. They still were sound asleep. Yet, there was something enormously different about the Master. A change had transpired in his own soul. He was now at peace even though they slept soundly. And for all of their apathy and indifference, he could say: "Sleep on now, and take your rest: behold, the hour is at hand, and the Son of man is betrayed into the hands of sinners" (Matt. 26:45).

Beneath it all we may see this: that Jesus steadfastly refused to manipulate men to his own advantage even in the hour of his bitterest need. He had the power to compel and coerce them but he knew that, while you may manipulate animals, you can never achieve anything good by manipulating men. You cannot remake them nor remold them. Only God can do that. If you are going to get along with difficult people, you will have to accept and bear with their limitations.

Cultivate Patience

In the second place, we must cultivate untiring patience. In the Bible patience means strong, persistent perseverance, the ability to bear with the limitations of others. A friend of mine tells about his seminary days when he worked at night in the post office to pay his expenses. Because of his superior background and ability, his supervisor said to him: "If you will work hard, I can give you a promotion and advance you over these who have worked here for years. You will be in an easy and comfortable position that will enable you to do some of your studying at night, and, perhaps, to get more sleep."

Stimulated and accelerated by the challenge, he began to run roughshod over his fellow workers. His job was to sort packages of mail and hand them to a woman who would stamp them and, in turn, throw them into a basket or box on the other side. To impress the supervisor, he worked furiously and stacked them far faster than the woman could stamp them. She became confused and said, "I am sorry, but I fear I have overlooked one of the packages. Would you mind digging it out of the box for me?" He left his assignment, found the package, and then furiously and frantically began to stack them higher and higher. Again she said, "I am very sorry, but I fear I have overlooked another one of the packages and I don't know which one it was. Could you help me find it?"

By that time his patience was exhausted. He said, "Why don't you quit?" With perfect calmness, she answered, "I know I am not very good at this job. I am slow and I'm hindering you. I'm standing in the way of your progress and of your promotion. But you will not work here very long and I must work here in this dull routine the rest of my life. Soon you will be out ministering in the name of Christ. Won't you learn to be a little more patient with us, for some of us are rather limited." Then she told the young man that one of her four children was ill, that she had scarcely slept for three days.

"I can hardly see these packages. My mind is dull. Won't you be a little more patient?"

God is always saying to superior people, "Your talent

came from me to be used to help those who are limited, and you are not to be impatient with them."

Control Your Resentment

Third, if we could get along with difficult people, we must learn to control our resentment. If ever a man had a right to be resentful it was Jesus of Nazareth. His family called him crazy. The religious authorities called him a blasphemer. The political powers said, "He is a rabble-rouser." He was deserted, denied, betrayed by his friends, beaten, spat upon, and finally, crucified.

But having loved his own, he loved them to the end. For the full strength of his soul is not revealed until you see him looking into the face of Judas, his own disciple, who comes now to betray him. Jesus calls him "friend." Finally, you see him upon the cross praying for his enemies.

Some time ago, I picked up a little volume called *Mere Christianity*, written by C. S. Lewis, onetime professor of Ancient and Medieval English at Cambridge, and one of the most powerful influences for Christ in Britain. It is a book that stimulates and makes Christianity exciting.

Lewis took the title from a statement of G. K. Chesterton that there is enough fire in mere Christianity to burn up everything that is mediocre in our souls. The author, talking about how we ought to love our enemies as ourselves, said that if we are going to learn to love our enemies, we must learn, first of all, how to love ourselves.

To love yourself is not necessarily to like yourself, though most of us have no difficulty there. But the truth is, every person who sees clearly at all into the deep crevices of his soul and understands anything of his personal motivation sees much within him that he doesn't like. There is always something there that he must loathe if he is sincere at all.

Yet, he continues to love himself, by which is meant, he continues to wish the very best for himself.

That is what our Lord meant when he commanded us to love our enemies. He wasn't talking about being fond of them or having any sort of affectionate feeling toward them. We cannot at any given moment compel ourselves to like someone who is obnoxious to us. Some people are by nature warm, demonstrative, affectionate, and some are always timid, distant, and cold. We cannot coerce our feelings. We *can* discipline them. Warmth may be cultivated.

Few things are more obnoxious than simulated affection. A Yale Divinity School professor required a term paper in which students were asked to explain the decline in status of the ministry. Some filled in pages, blaming it on science, insufficient education, or a divided church. One young man simply wrote four words: "His smiling, smiling face."

It is no sin to be somber and composed if that is your nature. Jesus wasn't talking about feeling when he told us to love our enemies. He was simply saying that we must want nothing but the best for others. If you really want only the best for others, this will prompt you to do something about it, for this kind of love must affect your will and motivate your actions.

Have you ever noticed that, while you might not like a person when you are doing nothing for him, if you will do something for him, you will begin to like him? While we are not commanded to like others, if we are to truly will the best for them, we must learn that it will be much easier to do that if we can learn to like them. It is said repeatedly in great devotional books that God loves the sinner but hates his sin. Again, C. S. Lewis said:

For a long time I used to think this a silly, straw-splitting distinction: how could you hate what a man did and not hate the man? But years later it occurred to me that there was one man to whom I had been doing this all my life—namely myself.[1]

Jesus surely knew that no man would ever completely measure up to his high ethical idealism. He never excluded any man from his company simply because he failed to measure up to the perfect standards of God. Those standards sit in judgment upon us and challenge us all our days. But the only power that lifts us toward them is the love of God which endures in spite of our failures. It is that love that draws us to him.

If you would get along with the most difficult of people, you must, first of all, begin with your own soul. Put down the rebellion and hostility against the highest which is within you. Fling open the gates to Christ and let him work that miracle of transformation which will help you to be happy in all your human relationships.

A Christian is one who knows that he is loved and, therefore, has enough security that he can afford to love all others.

12

What a Thankful Heart Can Do for You

Romans 1:8

*First, I thank my God through
Jesus Christ for you all, that your
faith is spoken of throughout the
whole world.*

The pathos of a self-centered, grasping, ungrateful heart is that it robs its owner of everything good which he truly desires in life. There is no greater proof of our depravity and twisted, distorted judgment than the fact that we allow our souls to be obsessed with the desire for things which we do not have and overlook the manifold blessings which are daily ours.

Gratitude is characteristic of a Christian heart. Paul never wrote a letter in which he did not, at the beginning, express gratitude or praise unto God. He was continually saying: "I thank my God through Jesus Christ." George Herbert has a prayer that ought to be always in our hearts:

O Lord, Thou hast given us so much;
Give us one thing more—
a grateful heart.[1]

The true measure of a man is in the measure of his gratitude and specifically in that for which he is most

80

thankful. If we thank God primarily for material things—food, raiment, automobiles, houses, and land—we are materialists. If we are most grateful for what God has done for us spiritually, we are rising higher on the scale of existence, yet, may still be supremely self-centered. If, however, we are most grateful for God himself, then we are of all men most blessed, for in having him we know that we shall have all things beside. "He that spared not his own Son, but delivered him up for us all, how shall he not with him also freely give us all things?" (Rom. 8:32).

A Thankful Heart Awakens Us

Blessings on the material and physical level come to mean most to us when we see them as tokens of God's wondrous love. And only to the grateful heart can they bring the fulness of their blessings. A thankful heart enlarges the mansions of our souls, for it does three things for us.

First, it makes us aware of an immeasurable heritage. Who can measure his personal debt to the Christian faith and lives of those who have gone before him? In countless ways our lives have been inspired, enriched, deepened, and strengthened by influences which have come out of the Christian loyalty and missionary zeal of the church in earlier days. Men who have faithfully served Christ through the church for more than a century look down upon us. It has often been said that our present generation is living on spiritual capital bequeathed by a previous age of faith.

The thankful heart enlarges the soul by making it continually aware of God's present goodness. The difference between a truly mature person and one who remains spiritually a child is that a baby considers all the world as his bottle to which he has an absolute right. The ungrateful person looks about him as though he were not a creature but a god with a right to all things. We forget the truth of the psalmist: "It is he that hath made us, and not we ourselves" (Psalm 100:3).

Dr. Lofton Hudson has written that when ingratitude, more strong than traitors' arms, lays hold on the hearts of men, they grumble, gripe, or grin, but never glow. Aldous Huxley once wrote that men don't spend their time thanking God for cars; they only curse when the carburetor is choked.

Finally, the thankful heart will make you generous. You cannot be truly thankful without wishing others to be thankful; so you share with them that for which you are most thankful, in order that they, too, may be thankful.

We have a gospel which cleanses man's immortal soul through forgiveness and regeneration, a gospel which restores man's lost fellowship with God and offers him life eternal. The only way we may demonstrate our gratitude for the gospel is by sharing it. If we are not grateful enough for it to share it, it is doubtful that we really have it. The very remembrance of what you have in Christ and of who you are without Christ must move you to share.

Remember Who You Are

Perhaps you have heard Roland Hayes, the Negro singer. His parents had been slaves. He was born in a tiny cabin in a former slave quarter of Georgia. His father died when he was but a boy, and he was brought up in penury without much opportunity, save that he had a good mother who reared him in a Christian home. When a music teacher heard him sing, doors began to open for him over all the world.

One of the highlights of Roland Hayes's experiences came in London. He was invited to sing before the King in Buckingham Palace. He was exhilarated. He sent an excited cablegram to his mother telling her about it. His mother cabled back four words that only a mother would ever think of sending: "Remember who you are." That, coming from a good mother, would deflate a young man, orient him, calm him, steady him. He went to Buckingham Palace remembering who he was.

As children of God, we must remember two things about ourselves: "It is he that hath made us, and not we ourselves." But we are children of the King of heaven. He has not been miserly with us, neither may we be miserly with him. You will not make your church, the body of the living Christ, a beggar on the doorstep of the world. Neither will you allow your pastors and your missionaries, who are servants of the Most High, to be regarded as paupers. When the word of God emphatically declares "the labourer is worthy of his hire" (Luke 10:7), you will respond accordingly.

George Bernard Shaw said that a gentleman is a man who puts back into life more than he takes out. Giving is a token of your trust. God has made it possible for you to give and to pledge to him. If you cannot believe that he will continue to prosper you as long as you continue to give, how can you believe that one day he will receive you into the high country of heaven?

Giving is the token of a kind and generous heart. Do you remember St. Augustine's description of the way he became a Christian? Ambrose won him to Christ. Years afterward, St. Augustine described his conversion by saying: "I began to love him, not at first as a teacher of the truth which I despaired of finding in thy church, but as a fellow creature who was kind to me." A fellow creature who was kind to me —that is real Christianity, not verbalized but acted. We may not win many St. Augustines from our city and our world but, by kindness expressed in giving, we can claim for

Christ, year after year, many a useful life. In days to come, when we are gone and by many forgotten, some may be thinking still, "I began to love him, not at first as a teacher of the truth which I despaired of finding in thy church, but as a fellow creature who was kind to me."

13

Preparing for the Unpredictable

James 4:14

*Whereas ye know not what shall
be on the morrow. For what is your
life? It is even a vapour, that
appeareth for a little time, and
then vanisheth away.*

Many college students are deeply enamored now
with the writings of the Nobel Prize winner, Albert Camus.
This great French writer has honestly and courageously
shattered the dreamworld of our fathers—that vapory, idealistic world that has crumbled upon its foundations. He has
gone straight through that world with the open, clean
confession that life is ultimately absurd, that there is no
reason behind, beneath, or beyond it, that it is sheer folly for
any man to try to predict the way his life will go.

Camus' own death seems a weird fulfilment of his conten-
tion. It was his plan to board a train for Paris, but influenced
by a comment of his friend, he took his car instead. Not long
thereafter, his mangled, motionless body was found
sprawled on the back seat of his car after he had attempted
to swing a curve at ninety miles an hour. The brightest light
in French literature went out in a moment and the Parisian
newspapers carried this headline: *Absurd!*

The Imponderable

It seems that the death of Camus strangely substantiates the belief that life is so riddled with incongruities that looking forward, not even the wisest can predict it and looking backward, not even the most experienced can find any coherence in it. If we believe that we are dependent solely upon reason, we, too, must admit that Camus was right, that life is ultimately absurd, that there is no reason in it, that no rationalistic philosopher ever yet has dissolved that dark enigma that haunts us as we live out our lives on this planet. No philosopher has ever yet told us from whence this ship of life was launched, why it is that we are on these troubled, turbulent waters, or where the ship shall cast her anchor at last. No philosopher can tell us whether our ship of life shall be sustained by the inextinguishable laughter of the sea or whether the storm will break and send us in a moment to the gray solitude of the bottom.

In our thoughtful moments we do find some sympathy with the sigh of the Brittany fisherman who cried, "O God, the sea is so wide and my little ship is so small!" Yet, incredible as this tiny ship and the bewildering vastness of the sea of life may be, still you and I do know some things about the ship. Most of us know our way to the common room of the ship where we spend much of our time in sophisticated banter, in furious patter, the kind of conversation in which we seek so desperately to parade the adequacy of our knowledge and wisdom. Still, if we will listen to ourselves for a moment, our own boisterousness betrays us. Our very loudness and the fact that we talk so much show how little security there is in our souls.

Most of us know the way to the engine room of the ship of life and we understand enough technology and electronics to know why it is that this ship of life stays in motion. Most of us know our way to the bar where, if life's mystery utterly overwhelms us, we can dull the edge of the soul until we silence the cry that comes from the deep and the call that comes from above.

But how few of us know our way to the deck of the ship. How few of us can find that place of quiet solitude where in silence we listen to those voices that speak only to the soul. It takes a rare kind of courage today to return the gaze of the stars. We can't bear to be that much alone with ourselves. We can't bear to understand the truth about ourselves, to stand in solitude when we seem to be searched by unseen eyes. We look out to the waters that are all around our vessel and the mystery is so overwhelming that there is nothing but darkness for us. We cry out in that blasé attitude that was so typical before the last world war: "One world at a time!"

The Unpredictable

But are not the heavens a part of our world? And who can think small thoughts while gazing at the heavens, or who can pour out his venomous profanity at the stars? And who is there who can look out on the vast, limitless expanse of the waters we must travel without having something of cold terror clutch at his heart?

A friend of mine, after spending a summer's vacation in Nassau, told of talking with a sailor assigned to the *Queen Elizabeth*. The seaman said, "No sailor is ever anything but afraid of the sea. He respects it. He knows how cruel the sea can be." You and I know how cruel the sea of life can be, but cruel, painful, unpredictable as it may be, this does not mean that it has no meaning. It may mean that the meaning of life's voyage is open only to the eyes of faith.

Camus, in his *Myth of Sisyphus,* said that the ultimate

question in life is whether or not to commit suicide. There isn't anything new about that. Hamlet said that three hundred years ago: "To be or not to be, that is the question." Camus admitted, as he examined the great depths of life, that there is something in life that makes its continuity more desirable than all the evils that assail life. The body has a brain, stronger than the mind at times, and it clings to life in spite of all of its afflictions. So Camus stated that even suicide may be absurd.

He calls attention to that postwar novelist who wrote a book, became uncertain about its merits, and then committed suicide to call attention to the book. He did succeed in calling attention to his book, but when it was read, it was judged of no value. All that Camus may be saying to us was said centuries ago to Christians. Christians have known for at least two thousand years that if you try to measure life solely through reason, it is ultimately absurd.

Who, for example, could hear the mother of Commander John Harvey of the submarine *Thresher*, as she addressed a nation-wide television audience, without being deeply moved when she said: "My hope is in God, for he is the God of the land and the sea and the sky." All hope already had been abandoned for the vessel. What could she say after all of these weeks of search by the Navy, when no one yet knows what happened to that supposedly unsinkable ship? If Mrs. Harvey had lived by the rules of reason, then she, out of obligation to reason, would have had to abandon her faith. But as it was, her loss only added another dimension to her faith, and she came in time to see that even if her boy went down at sea, he was at least going down into the open arms of God.

You and I are such children. We are enamored with our own wisdom. We are children pondering the imponderable.

There is too much sorrow in this world for the human mind to sustain, to read meaning into or out of. So here we are with this vast, dark abyss before all our earthly days and at the close of our earthly days, and we ask the black, bewildering question of the enigma of life: Is anything predictable?

Think first of the human, physical side of life. You read of the sudden death of an all-American football player, a magnificent man of muscle and mighty physique. Who would have dreamed that in a sudden moment he could have been utterly destroyed by the insidious disease called leukemia? Or think of the mental life, how unpredictable it is. Here is a great writer conversing until late in the night with his colleagues. His mind is more perceptive and brilliant than any of those about him. But on the morrow, when he awakens, it is to a strange, new world, totally different from the world he knew the night before, for he has lost touch with reality.

Or think how unpredictable is our social life. Here is a man who comes to his pastor after many years of marriage and says, "I didn't dream there was anything wrong, but suddenly yesterday afternoon, I was presented with divorce papers and with an injunction forbidding me to talk to my wife or even to return to my home." Think how unpredictable the economic world is. Here is a man who gives half of his years to a certain company. The business now is sold. New personnel comes in to replace the man. His training is for only one job and at his age he can find no further employment. How can he believe anything, save that life is so capricious it doesn't care for him?

Prepare for the Unpredictable

Is there anything we can do to buttress ourselves against the unpredictable side of life? Is Christian faith more than blind obedience to fate, the belief that ultimately all things will be balanced out to the believer?

First, you can know that God is not responsible for the unpredictable evils of life. Our religion is often twisted and distorted, simply because we make God responsible for the very things from which he is seeking to deliver us. We are guilty of entangling our lives. We find our guilt so intolerable that we want to transfer it to someone else, so we try to make God responsible for it.

The evils of this earth are not from God. They are the result of the imbalance in the universe caused by human sin and rebellion against the eternal. Basic in all our Christian belief is the fact that God is doing all within his power to bring this world back into balance, to rid us of our evil, to restore our souls. If we can't believe that, there is little hope for us.

We do not believe in God simply because all things are bright and beautiful and because all things go smoothly for us. We believe in God because there is more reason for believing in him than there is for not believing in him. There is a problem of good in our world as well as a problem of evil. No matter how dark and difficult our days, there has always been more of sunshine than of shadow, more of good than evil, more of light than of darkness. How can you account for the preponderance of good in your life and in your world if there is no God? Here then is the first thing: Believe that God is not responsible for evil. You and an evil world have made possible your suffering—not God.

Facing Ultimate Questions

The second question is: Is faith simply the blind submission to the belief that life will finally be balanced out for the believer? That philosophy was in this world long before

Christ was born. It is the stoic philosophy and it has very little in it that is akin to Christianity. Christianity, on the other hand, is the belief in the God made real to us in Christ, the God of love whose power is beneath his love and behind his merciful purpose for every man. To have that faith you must begin with the humble admission that you do not know all the answers. The truth is, you don't know many of the answers. The greater truth is that you don't even know the important questions of life. The reason we are so bewildered is that we are always preoccupied with the wrong questions.

Only Christ, of all men who ever walked this earth, knew the ultimate questions of life. If you want to see him as he asks the final, the most important of all questions, behold him in the last hour of agony upon the cross of Calvary. Nothing is left now save his dying breath. Through it all he ventures with faith, for he walks as a man would walk. He hangs upon the cross in human frailty. There is no light, nothing but darkness, and nothing will come through to him save that which comes through his faith. Here is the bottom of human darkness. Here the iron chains shackle the soul in this narrow sphere of the senses.

He faces the full fury of evil and goes into that darkness which has shut out the light of all stars and trembles on the brink of the one great alternative: is it annihilation or is it the open arms of God? He cries out the one important question, "My God, my God, why hast thou forsaken me?" (Matt: 27:46).

There is no evidence that anything is working for him in deliverance. There is nothing but darkness and anguish and agony and no reason running through it all. His question means this: "If what I have taught men about God is true, if the God that I revealed to humanity is true, then he cannot forsake me now." So he trembles with the horrible alternative that possibly there will be no answer to that question. He will not play us false. He did not offer an easy religion. He came not to talk about death but to die and go into death and into judgment to face the ultimates of heaven and hell. He faces them in faith, the faith that out there somewhere there are hands. So he cries out at last and as he reaches into the darkness he feels hands. They are the hands of God. His final word is, "Father, into thy hands I commend my spirit" (Luke 23:46).

In that love that was laid bare on Calvary, your ship of life was launched. On the bosom of the great deep your ship of life must sail, for it is the bosom of God. In those open arms of God your ship at last will drop anchor. You can prepare for life's unpredictables only by firming up your faith in God.

I have reread lately that wonderful autobiography of Joseph Fort Newton, *River of Years*. In it he tells of a word of wisdom sent him by an old friend on a New Year's card:

. . . hope much, fear not at all, love with all your heart, do your best, seek the best in others; take life and dare it, have a little fun and share it; and put your trust in "the veiled kindness of the Father of men," in whose great hand we stand.[1]

14

When Your Heart Is Troubled

John 14:1

Let not your heart be troubled: ye
believe in God, believe also in me.

On the pinnacle of Mount Zion is a room reached
by a steep and toilsome stairway. It is appropriately called
the upper room. For many centuries troubled hearts have
turned to this room for consolation. Dearer to the heavy
laden than any shrine in Christendom is this upper room.

Here Jesus found peace when he stood on the threshold of
Calvary. Here he broke the bread and drank from the cup
with those whom God had called out of the world that,
through sunshine and cloud, they might cling to him. Here
these men, who had traveled down the years with him and
loved him most passionately, pledged to be true to him until,
beyond life's last shadow, they sat with him at the banquet
above.

In this upper room Jesus promised them another com-
forter and spoke those deathless words about the Father's
house of many mansions. The Upper Room has always been
the refuge of the faithful. After Calvary had ravaged the
hearts of the disciples, they turned their weary footsteps
back to the upper room and found refuge from the murder-

ous mob. Here, at last, their mourning was turned into wild, incredulous joy as Jesus walked through the locked door.

In all likelihood, it was here that the Holy Spirit came down in the glory of Pentecost and the Christian church was born. To this room every Christian heart returns in his hour of bereavement.

Some months ago, I stood with a fellow pastor to conduct the funeral of a young man forty-four years of age, the father of a seven-year-old and a sixteen-year-old boy. In the service the pastor told of two ministers whose wives had died very close together. One of them reacted by saying: "For me, the world has tumbled in!" The other responded by saying: "For me, the heavens have opened!" The former is the reaction of despair and the latter of trust. It is the mission of the church to prepare her communicants to see courageously the heavens open in moments of bereavement.

The Meaning of Trouble

From that upper room, in the long ago and far away, came words which our Lord would still lift before every sorrowing heart: "Let not your heart be troubled." J. B. Phillips puts it: "You must not let yourselves be distressed."

What did he mean?

Surely he did not mean, do not let your heart be shaken! He could not have been very sincere or consistent if that is what he meant. At the grave of Lazarus this very same word, which is here translated troubled, was used of Jesus' attitude: "He groaned in the spirit, and was troubled" (John 11:33). His heart was stirred and shaken.

Neither did he mean, let not your heart care or be concerned. Are we not commanded to bear one another's burdens?

It could not mean, let not your tears fall. Did not Jesus

weep at the grave of his friend? Are not tears heaven's healing balm when the great deeps of life are broken up within us?

It could not mean, do not be bewildered. Jesus was bewildered in the presence of the cross. In his prayer, he confessed this to his Father: "Now is my soul troubled; and what shall I say?" (John 12:27).

Jesus was not offering impossible counsel nor showing an easy way out of bereavement. He was far too honest and compassionate to add to our human burden advice which no man can follow.

What then did he mean?

First, don't let your soul be shattered by fear. You will be afraid but don't let fear unhinge your faith and your reason. Real religion rallies our souls around the truth that if the worst does come, there is really nothing to be ultimately afraid of. Christ is still in control.

Jesus' disciples feared even their own Master! In Matthew 14:26, when the disciples saw him walking on the water, "they were troubled, saying, It is a spirit." Their fears were unfounded. They had thought that their dearest friend was a hostile spirit.

What a strong paradox it is that people are troubled both by the coming of Jesus and the departure of Jesus. In Matthew 2:3, we are told that when Herod received the word from the Wise Men that a "King of the Jews" had been born, "he was troubled, and all Jerusalem with him." He was *tarasso* (troubled).

Others were also troubled in the wake of the announcement of Jesus in John 13:33: "Little children, yet a little while I am with you. Ye shall seek me: and as I said unto the Jews, Whither I go, ye cannot come." When the Wise Men first went up to worship Jesus, Herod trembled and all

Jerusalem, and when Jesus announced his departure from the earth, again men trembled.

Well may we tremble at his coming if we are out of harmony with him. And well may we say with the poet:

> But in this boasted march of wrong and error,
>   'Mid the vast splendor of an age that glows,
> One thing, O Jesus, fills my heart with terror;
>   The echo of Thy voice still feebler grows.[1]

It is rational to fear both the coming and the departure of Jesus. Still, our Lord was here saying, "Don't let imaginary fears clutch at your heart with their cold, cold hands. I will never really leave you nor forsake you. My departure from the life of the flesh is only that I may be nearer to you forever."

Jesus prayed, "Now is my soul troubled; and what shall I say? Father, save me from this hour: but for this cause came I unto this hour: . . . Father, glorify thy name" (John 12:27–28). He was acknowledging that the soul's hour of testing was also the supreme opportunity to glorify God.

Only Believe

Look then at how the troubled heart is put to rest.

The antidote of fear is trust. "Ye believe in God," said Jesus, "believe also in me" (John 14:1). "I have always cared for you and will never cease to care for you. My very going from you is the supreme proof of how much I care. The cross will open up for you my kingdom of love."

In the Middle Ages, a monk announced that he would preach a sermon on the love of God. When the people gathered in the cathedral and waited in silence, through the magnificent windows the last rays of the dying sun filtered. As all the color faded and the darkness came down, the monk took a lighted candle from the candelbra and carried it to the full-sized statue of the Christ upon the cross. He held the light beneath the wounds of his feet, then moved it to his hands and then to his side. In complete silence, he let the light shine on the thorn-crowned brow. No word was spoken in that sermon. Yet, everyone understood that they were in the presence of a great mystery beyond description. They were beholding the dimensions of a love beyond man's power to measure.

Again, the heart lies down in rest and peace when we trust the provisions of God. Jesus said, "In my Father's house are many mansions [*monai*—abiding places]" (John 14:2). This word has three possible meanings, as William Barclay so ably indicates.

The Jews believed in "ranks of blessedness" which were assigned according to the measure of a person's goodness. In the *Book of the Secrets of Enoch,* it is written that in the world to come there are many mansions prepared for men, good for good, evil for evil. Each is assigned a room such as his life has merited.

The Greeks thought of *monai* as stages of development. Pausanias wrote, "*Monai* means stages—progress—advance —development." Heaven is not a static condition. Origen believed that when a man died, his soul went to some place called "paradise." There he received training and teaching and when he was worthy of it and fit for it, his soul ascended into the air, passing through various stages (monai) which the Greeks called "spheres" and the Jews called "heavens." Through these they would pass until they reached the final heaven. The writer of Hebrews saw the soul following Jesus who "passed into the heavens" (4:14). These writers could not imagine the soul bursting into the full splendor of heaven in a moment.

The meaning of *monai* may be far simpler than either of the above suggestions. It may be that Jesus is simply saying, "In heaven there is room for all. Your earthly tenements become very crowded. Don't be afraid; the great bounty of God is adequate for you."

What a word is this for those of us who fear the population explosion which overtaxes our planet! "Men may shut their doors on you here but remember that the city of God has twelve gates. You will not have to wait for an entrance. As you preach," Jesus said to his own, "they will slam the door in your faces as they did to me. But in heaven you will never be shut out."

In one of J. M. Barrie's books is the story of Jess and her little son, Joey. It was Joey's ambition to be a minister. Often he told his mother that when he preached his first sermon, he was going to use the text that he loved best of all, namely, "Thou God seest me" (Gen. 16:13). But one black day Joey was killed by a passing cart almost in his mother's door. Then the bitterness of death settled around Jess until she could not think of those words, "Thou God seest me."

After months and years had passed, she said that on the day her son was buried, she could not bear to think that God was looking on. But now those words, "Thou God seest me," had become her favorite scripture verse. She said that she found herself turning up the passage in the Bible more often than any other and reading the whole chapter. When she came to the words, "Thou God seest me," she let the book lie upon her lap, for she knew that once a person is sure of that, he is sure of everything.

God sees, God knows, God cares, God loves, God has also provided. When a person believes that, his heart can lie down and rest.

15

Is There Any Hope?

1 Corinthians 15:19–20

If in this life only we have hope in Christ, we are of all men most miserable. But now is Christ risen from the dead, and become the firstfruits of them that slept.

Some time ago, the world was startled by the headlines: LITTLE HOPE! You read the tragic story of the $45,000,000 nuclear submarine, *Thresher*, that went down 220 miles off the coast of Boston, carrying 129 men. If you did as I, you ran hastily down the column reading the names to find if any were from your hometown. As I did this, I thought of how small-minded I was being. I returned to reading the column more carefully and reverently, for every one of these was known and loved of God and each man had given his life for his country.

Lt. Ronald C. Babcock, Portsmouth, New Hampshire; Ronald C. Bain, Mount Vernon, Illinois; John E. Bell, Mystic, Connecticut. On and on I read until my thoughts turned to another sea disaster not many years ago when, off the coast of Massachusetts, the submarine *S-4* went down. It had been rammed, and divers went down to attempt a rescue. As they drew near the vessel, they heard tappings from within. With great difficulty they made out the Morse code letter by letter: I–S T–H–E–R–E A–N–Y H–O–P–E–?

Is there any hope? rang out from the depths of the sea. From the depths of the souls of men there comes that same call that has come out of all our human anguish for many centuries. Is there any hope?

The Importance of Easter

If the Easter gospel is not true, if what we celebrate on this holy day which has inspired the noblest thoughts of Western man for two thousand years is nothing but pretentious, pagan ceremony, let us put it exactly where Paul put it. Paul was a tough-minded realist. He wrote these words in letters of iron on the granite face of time: "If Christ be not raised, your faith is vain; ye are yet in your sins. Then they also which are fallen asleep in Christ are perished" (1 Cor. 15:17–18). There is no hope if what we celebrate at Easter is not true.

Shortly before Easter some years ago, a mother and father returned from the cemetery where they had buried their fourteen-year-old son, who had died from diphtheria. In those days there was little help for that dreaded disease. Returning to their home, they were further shattered by the news that another child had died and only the three-year-old remained.

The following day they went back to the house of God to observe another funeral ceremony. The congregation stood to lift up an ancient hymn of Christian hope, but the father was too benumbed of soul to sing. The beautiful mother put her hand upon his as they rose to repeat the Apostles' Creed and he summoned his strength and was able to say those deathless words: "I believe in God the Father Almighty, Maker of heaven and earth: And in Jesus Christ his only Son our Lord; . . . I believe in the Holy Ghost: The holy Catholic Church; . . . The Resurrection of the body; And the Life everlasting." In the mere repeating of those words, there came a strange strength back into his soul so that he walked out of that church with colossal courage. A little boy, who had watched the bereaved parents all through the service, turned to his father and said, "You know, they really believe it, don't they?" "Believe what?" asked the father. "The whole big thing," said the boy, "the whole big thing about Easter."

It is a big thing. It is the biggest thing of time and eternity, of heaven and earth. It is too big to be left to our intellects. There must be a word from God concerning this. The word must be more than a vocal word; it must be a living demonstration of divine power. So that word comes through and is laid bare in the garden of the resurrection. "But now is Christ risen from the dead, and become the firstfruits of them that slept." The firstfruits—the harbinger of the full and final harvest.

Nevertheless We Live

It is a very rare thing that any man past fifty years of age ever comes to me anymore to talk about death. As we grow older, we imagine we are brave and courageous and, therefore, we do not have to talk about this dread subject anymore. But often I feel our silence is but a subterfuge of deep, repressed terror—the refusal to truly face the grim reality and draw strength from above.

Strangely, this silence is not characteristic of young people. You would think when the heart is young and the strength is at its full tide and there is every reason to live, young people would not be concerned about this. But next to the deep moral problems, I talk with college students more about death these days than about anything else. I am certain that the reason they read the works of Camus is because he has dealt so realistically with the great futility of life. If life ends in the grim, greedy, muddy ditch called the grave, what meaning can one ever find in it?

I wonder if you know that one of the major mental problems of our world is the problem of suicide for people under twenty years of age? It is growing rapidly now in France. In statistics released recently from Paris, we were told that 6,923 French youths took their lives in 1960, compared with the previous year of 7,571, and since the year 1952, the figure has never fallen below 6,500. Because it was such an appalling phenomenon, the Sixth Annual International Congress of Mental Health decided to investigate. Congress' report uncovered the reason why young people take their own lives. The first was romantic disappointment, then family discord, then professional failure either at school or at work, and finally, the sorrow over the death of someone. Young people look realistically at one truth—that unless there is a hope of reunion, there is no assuaging of the sorrow of the human soul over death.

James McConoughy tells of one of our missionaries in Korea who sat at the bedside of his beautiful wife as she slipped out into the sleep that knows no earthly waking. His heart was utterly crushed. She had been his companion for fifteen years, and knowing what it meant to him, she said, "Don't grieve, dear, you'll get me back." Four months went by. He sat at the bedside of his little boy who was also going down into death. He could not restrain the tears until the little boy said, "Don't cry, Daddy, you'll get me back."

As they bore the little body out to the burial ground, the Koreans gathered around and they, too, were in tears until one of them turned upon his own friends and said, "Why are you weeping?" They answered, "Because the foreigner has lost his little boy!" "Well, weep for yourselves," said he, "you have lost sons and you will never get them back. I have lost a little girl and I will never get her back. But these foreigners have a strange way of getting back their dead!"

The strange way is the cross. Have you ever thought of the cross as the shaft of God, shoved down vertically from the heavens into the depths of the realm of death to serve as a lever to lift us back into the fellowship of God? It is the vertical pole of the cross let down from above which sustains the church, the community of the resurrection. The church represents the horizontal arms of the cross through which Christ still reaches out to enfold this world to his heart, to bring it into life eternal. That is what Jesus meant when he said, "I, if I be lifted up from the earth, will draw all men unto me" (John 12:32). By that cross he banishes the last great sarcasm of life, which is death.

Michael Farraday, one of the greatest of all scientists, stood one time at the grave of a peasant. There he saw a chrysalis suddenly open and a beautiful butterfly emerge. It was such a lovely parable of the resurrection, he could not restrain tears. When he died, he ordered that the image of a broken chrysalis should be placed upon his tombstone and beneath it the words, "Nevertheless I live" (Gal. 2:20).

More Than Survival

A final thought is this: we are not talking primarily about survival. As I gathered a group of young ministerial students about me some time ago, they began to talk about man's strange concept that survival will solve all of his problems. Somehow we think, concerning our physical health, that if we can only survive the ordeal of suffering then tomorrow will be better and we will be stronger physically; if we can only live long enough, we will outgrow all of our moral handicaps. No serious thinker really believes that. We know that survival does not solve anything. If we were simply talking about a life that goes on and on and on and is no different from the life we know here, if life were to be as glum and dismal for some of us on the other side as it is here, I think some of us would pray for annihilation, for going down into that pit where the wicked cease from troubling and the weary are at rest.

The Christian doctrine of the resurrection is not simply a doctrine of survival. It is the doctrine of the lifting of the totality of human personality into a better life, a rebirth, a birth from above and into the image of Christ. When that happens, life becomes worthy of this everlasting dimension. Resurrection is not only the lifting of life but the transformation of our environment. This is what Paul meant when he said, "The whole creation groaneth and travaileth in pain. . . . waiting for the adoption, to wit, the redemption of our body" (Rom. 8:22–23).

An old sea captain was far out to sea when the storm came up, and the mist came down so close around the vessel that before he could swing it about the night had lowered. There were no stars. In those days there was no radar, no steam engine to power a vessel, nothing but the wind to move the little boat, and the wind must catch the sails. When for many days neither sun, moon, nor stars appeared, he could do nothing but trust those sails to the gales of God. Then, one day, a ray of light broke through and the sun began to burn away the mist until the fog was lifted, and he saw the beautiful harbor of Rio de Janeiro.

Some day, beyond life's storms, the mist will be lifted and we will see the city of God and we will be at home and shall sing those words that our fathers sang, "I shall see the land of Beulah with mine eyes undimmed by tears." But you say,

"Wherein is our assurance that this shall happen? I don't know much about theology, and I don't know anything about eschatology. Wherein is our assurance?" Well, it is in one shining truth: Christ so loved us that he broke the bonds of death to stand beside us. He came walking to his own on the troubled waters. He still walks to us on our troubled waters.

To me, the most beautiful symbolism of what Christ does for us in the storm is in that story of his walking on the water. I know that we moderns are not very much at home in the realm of the miraculous. We are embarrassed when anything comes to us that upsets our neat little pattern of this ordered universe, anything beyond our grasp. We do not want anyone disturbing that little segment of knowledge which we have gained. So we discard the miracles. But you cannot discard this—the deeper miracle of what happened in the souls of those apostles!

Christ was praying, and it is said that he was alone in prayer. He was on the mountain alone. But Jesus was never really alone, not even when he prayed. He never looked into the face of the Father without seeing also those whom he loved, and in that communion of prayer there came through to him the truth that his own were in trouble. They were caught in the storm at sea. He not only prayed for them, he went to them. Between him and them lay the turbulent waters of deep, blue Gennesaret. But love would find a way. Nothing would stop him. He walked across those waters and when they saw him they were terrified. They thought he was a ghost, for in those days everyone believed in ghosts. Jesus said to them, "Take courage, be not afraid, it is I." But try as they would, they could not let go and get hold of their fears. Finally, Jesus climbed into the boat beside them and it is said that the wind dropped.

Have you ever thought of the strange, mysterious power of the touch of one human life upon another, of one human body upon another, the touch of man with man, of man with woman, with mysterious powers and strange personal forces that go down beneath the region and level of intellect? Suppose you saw a child that was very afraid, so panic-stricken that the features of his face were frozen. What would you say to him? "Don't be afraid"? If you were wise at all, you would say nothing. You would take his hand. You would put your arm around him and then there would come healing.

So here is the meaning of the story of Christ walking on the water. He prayed for his own, but even that did not curb the wind. The storm did not drop and their fears were not allayed by his prayers. He walked to them but even his miracle only heightened their fear. He gave them his finest word of courage and comfort but that was not enough. He got into the boat beside them and the wind dropped.

16

More Than Immortality

2 Timothy 1:10

Our Saviour Jesus Christ, who hath abolished death, and hath brought life and immortality to light through the gospel.

"If a man die, shall he live again?" (Job 14:14). This is a question which has plagued civilized man since time began. There have been different attitudes toward it. For example, first there is the attitude of the agnostic voiced by Socrates in his *Apologia* when he said, "We go our separate ways, I to die, you to live. Which is better, God only knows." But although many have doubted, most have believed in the continuity of life after death.

Although the belief is sometimes crudely expressed, it is nonetheless real. The Moslem's paradise, for example, is the apotheosis of material delight. He is told that if in this life he is righteous, when death comes he will be transported to a magnificent palace, will be given eighty thousand servants, will be served a dinner of three hundred courses, will be given a bevy of seventy-two gorgeous wives endowed with perpetual youth and beauty, and will himself be endowed with perpetual youth.

The Greeks believed in immortality. They saw their gods

on Mount Olympus sipping wine from golden goblets, hurling thunderbolts at one another, and stealing one another's wives. Greek demigods dwelt in the Elysian fields; and below the earth, in the dark, dismal regions where a wraithlike existence went on and on and on, was a realm called Hades which all mortals enter at death. Above its entrance were these words: "Abandon hope, all ye who enter here!" Immortality was real, but it was not morally significant. There was personal survival, but there was no hope of anything better.

All Orientals have believed in the continuity of life after death. Buddha taught that through the negation of desire, one could achieve a state of nirvana and cease to desire anything. It is not hard to understand why the Oriental wanted such a curtailed existence, for in that heavily over-populated world where disease was rampant, famines were rife, and life was hard and grew more dreary with every passing day, life was a liability. Do you marvel then that the Oriental longed for the cessation of existence as his immortality? His major problem, even in his religion, was how he could get rid of an existence beyond the grave.

The American Indian believed in immortality. I shall long remember that day when, after preaching in the First Baptist Church in Muskogee, Oklahoma, I went out to a little Indian village where stands Bacone College. There I met an Indian artist, Dick West, a great artist who has painted some of the most magnificent works of western art. He told me of the Indian's belief in the trail in the sky which he would follow after death until he came at last to the happy hunting ground. He buried his bow and arrows in the grave with him. His dog also was buried there that he might run the deer without weariness in the land of eternal sky-blue water and fadeless day.

An Anchor for Hope

To gather in the house of God once a year on Easter morning in order to pay one's bland respect to the doctrine of immortality no more makes a man a Christian than was Pontius Pilate, for he too believed in immortality. So did the Pharisees who crucified Jesus. In fact, very few of the world's most ruthless people have refused to believe in immortality. Doubting it is only a modern fad.

All this I say to emphasize the truth that the coming of Jesus of Nazareth into our world did not give to humanity the belief in immortality. Man had that centuries before Jesus was born in Bethlehem of Judea. But this much our Lord and Master did for us. He enabled us to remove from the realm of speculative philosophy the basis of our belief in immortality and to anchor it deep in a concrete, historic event—the bodily resurrection of the Man of Nazareth. He enables us to sing with Richard Baxter:

> My knowledge of that life is small,
> The eye of faith is dim;
> But 'tis enough that Christ knows all,
> And I shall be with Him.[1]

So Jesus directed this hope and made personal this belief in three areas: in his teaching, in his life, and in his death and resurrection.

I mention first his teaching, for Jesus declared unequivocally the universal Fatherhood of God and its grand corollary, the brotherhood of man. He saw in the fusion of these two the perfect righteous order which one day, by the grace of God, would come. He saw a just order upon the earth which he called the kingdom of God in its earthly dimension. In that kingdom he magnified nothing quite so much as the value of human personality. He said: "So valuable are you that the very hairs of your heads are numbered before God" (cf. Matt. 10:30).

He said, "Man is a child of God, potentially destined for eternal fellowship with the Father; therefore, man can only derive his true direction in life by emulating the character of God." God is compassionate; therefore, what can we do but be kind to one another? God is impartial in his goodness. "He maketh his sun to rise on the evil and on the good, and sendeth rain on the just and on the unjust" (5:45). How dare we then ever ask about the merit of man? We too must do good to all men. God is absolutely uncompromising in his righteousness. We dare not refuse to oppose evil wherever it is found in this world and however unpopular it may be.

The genius of the Man of Nazareth was that he never tried to practice what he preached. He preached what he practiced! There is a vast difference. This is the reason he was perfectly natural and at home here. He felt that this is God's world. He felt no deep insecurity in being in the presence of publicans and sinners. What cared he if those religious leaders said, "Why, he associates with the underworld! He even has among his companions a woman from the underworld!" Jesus felt no disgrace over sitting at the well, talking with a fallen woman. He was so far from being a recluse that little children, who are the best judges of character, ran instinctively into his arms. I think he could have joined heartily in singing that wondrous hymn of childhood, written by M. D. Babcock:

> This is my Father's world,
>   And to my listening ears,
> All nature sings, and round me rings
>   The music of the spheres.

· ·

This is my Father's world,
The battle is not done;
Jesus who died shall be satisfied,
And earth and heaven be one.[2]

Our Lord also established the basis for all authority on this earth when they came to him to ask, "Who is the authority, God or Caesar?" To Jesus this was not an either-or question, but a both-and question. He replied, "Render therefore unto Caesar the things which are Caesar's; and unto God the things that are God's" (22:21). Then he said, "But you must remember that the final authority is spiritual, for all other authorities pass away."

Our little systems have their day;
They have their day and cease to be:
They are but broken lights of Thee,
And Thou, O Lord, are more than they.[3]

His life did not quite fit the picture of the religion of the times. The Sadducees, the intelligentsia, were those who had succeeded in throwing aside all the traditions of their fathers. If they had any religion at all, it was in the open denial of established religion. They said, "We cannot accept anything save that which fits neatly now within the confines of our present lives." So, they did not believe in angels. They did not believe in the resurrection.

They came to Jesus one day with a hypothetical question, an insincere question, a question designed to engage the Lord in controversy, a question predicated on that ancient tribal law placed upon the statutes of Israel during her Bedouin days. In those days, Israel practiced polygamy for the same reason that all ancient peoples practiced polygamy, for the maintenance of a high birthrate and for assuring the strength of the tribe. In those fierce days of tribal wars, when men were constantly killed, there were few men and many women and no means of caring for women on the desert. So there was placed on the statutes of Israel the law requiring a man whose brother had been killed in battle to take his wife into his tent and make a home for her. It was not a moral matter but an economic matter.

So said the Sadducees, "Here is a woman who has been the wife of seven husbands. Seven men have been killed in battle and she has been passed from one brother to another until she has had seven husbands. Now, in the resurrection, whose wife will she be?" (cf. Matt. 22:24–28). Remember that they did not believe she would be anybody's wife for they did not believe in the resurrection. Jesus said, "You do greatly err, not knowing the power of God. Have you never read the word of God? I am the God of Abraham, the God of Isaac, and the God of Jacob. These men have been dead for hundreds of years. I am not the God of the dead, but of the living" (cf. 29–32). In other words, those upon whom God has set his affection will never die.

God's Consistency

So Jesus cut across every philosophical corollary and established the basis for believing in the life eternal, not on the budding of the branches nor the blooming of the lilies nor the glories of the springtime. Beautiful and lovely analogies though they be, they are never anything more than that. Jesus established his belief in the life eternal on his doctrine of God. "What do you believe about God?" he asked. "Do you believe that he is one that would love you into existence, hold your hand all across the grim pilgrimage of earth until you come to a greedy, muddy ditch called the grave, only to see you fall in and then turn his back upon you forever?" Jesus did not believe that, and his followers did not believe it either. They believed that when the shadows gathered, they would not walk into the valley alone, but that out beyond the dark valley would stand the Shepherd with his staff and rod.

Then came the time when all their dreams were destroyed, for Jesus died. These disciples had nothing left. Their dreams were utterly shattered and apparently, not one of them believed that Jesus would come out of the grave. Simon Peter, who was to be the leader of the apostolic band, said, "It is all over and I am going back to the old fishing business." So they all decided to go with him. They were disillusioned and their faith was in eclipse—until the resurrection morning.

Remember that the resurrection of Jesus had been both the most doubted doctrine of earth and at the same time the most firmly established truth in the Christian faith. There are two lines of evidence that support it. First, the external evidence. Saul of Tarsus was transformed from the great persecutor of the faith to the formulator of the Christian doctrine because he met the risen Man of Nazareth walking outside the gates of Damascus. Paul the apostle said, "Most of them who beheld him are still alive. If you do not believe what I am telling you, go and ask them." Five of the writers of the New Testament tell the resurrection story, and five hundred of the brethren saw our Lord alive from the dead.

There is also enduring evidence that is more than historical. How do you think it ever came about that so many intelligent people should gather so constantly in your own house of worship on the Lord's Day? They are not alone. Multiplied millions gather with them across the earth to testify that they have entered the communion of the resurrection of Jesus. To them the most real presence of earth is the presence of the risen Christ who meets with them wherever they gather.

You then say, "My scientific mind will not go with you there. How can I believe and what difference will it make?" It will make all the difference in the world. You cannot have any measure of Christian faith if you do not believe this. We cannot equivocate here! Jesus said that in his death he would go down and in three days he would rise again. If he was wrong there, perhaps he was wrong in everything else he said. Why trust him at all if you do not trust him here? This trust will make all the difference in the world, for no generation has known so many open graves, so many empty chairs, so many aching voids as has ours. And when you put your trust in Christ, you begin to see that it has some scientific validity.

Life Everlasting

Biologists tell us that every five to seven years our bodies deteriorate. This process does not destroy us. Our personalities go on. Why should that which happens instantaneously, which we call physical death, do any more to destroy the soul of man than that which is occurring every moment that we live? Jesus taught that we have already begun to live eternally and that what we shall be in eternity, we are rapidly becoming. We had better look seriously at that. Death will not transform our desires. What you want most now may be what you shall desire most in eternity.

You remember Tennyson's dear friend, Arthur Hallam, who died and for a long season the faith of the great poet was in eclipse because he felt that his friend would go on developing utterly unimpaired by the body, and he would never be able to catch up with him. Then he found comfort in the fact that he could live so close to God down here that when he too passed over, he would be within hailing distance of his friend.

Victor Hugo made Jean Valjean say, "It is nothing to die. It is an awful thing never to have lived." Mark Guy Pierce, the great British preacher, who died in his thirty-seventh year, asked his friends to bury him at the altar where he had seen so many bury the old life of sin and rise to walk in newness of life—and to play not the death march but "Gloria," and to sing "Praise God"—and somewhere, he would be singing with them.

We may well close our meditation with thanksgiving unto God for Jesus Christ who has abolished death and has brought life and immortality to light through the gospel and who has given us a life that death can never sever and the grave can never end.

For the Preacher

17

Putting People Back Together

1 Corinthians 14:3

*But he who preaches the word of
God is using his speech for the
building up of the faith of one man,
the encouragement of another or
the consolation of another
(Phillips).*

She was not a brilliant girl and far from being
attractive. How could she be? She had suddenly seen her
world collapse about her. When my secretary brought her
into my office, she was so shocked and ashamed that she
would not even give me her name. She said, "I have just
come from the bridge behind your church. I was ready to
jump when I looked up and saw the spire. I decided to come
and see if there was anything under that spire to prevent my
returning to the bridge."

Then, she unfolded an unbelievably sordid and tragic
drama. She was a student at a nearby college. Tomorrow she
was to have her final exams. That morning the word had
come from a northern city that her father had killed her
mother, her mother's paramour, and himself. When she left
my office she was feeling little better. But she said, "I don't
know what I am going to do but I'm not going back to the
bridge."

Do you wonder what I talked about with her? Well, all

the easy answers and smooth clichés took flight and I found myself breathing a prayer to God for wisdom. Every human analogy I knew broke down and, for the first time in my ministry, I came upon a central truth in the gospel. Suppose I had said to her, "God is your Father; you must trust him; he loves you and will allow no final harm to come to you." How could she ever trust a father again? Her father had shattered her world and all her dreams.

Then it came to me that God is not a father like her father or my father. He is the Father of our Lord and Saviour, Jesus Christ, and this is the only place where the analogy fits. God is not like your father unless your father has qualities derived from a personal relationship with Christ. So I talked to her about the Saviour whose love is above all human love, who shares our heartbreak and can bring us through, not without scars, but with souls that are stronger than they could ever have been otherwise. A pastor's primary responsibility is not to justify suffering but to help people use it creatively. How can our preaching do this?

The Center of the Gospel

A competent, contemporary preacher I have heard defines preaching as "rubbing up against the rough edges of a man's soul with the gospel." Now, if he meant that we are to allow the gospel to sit in judgment upon our waywardness and wandering, to call us back into the only kind of existence in which life is bearable, I would endorse his definition. Unfortunately, too many of us add private abrasives to our preaching which only irritate and repel and drive people away from the fountain of healing waters.

Too much of our own inadequacy and impropriety gets into the modern pulpit and distorts the gospel. Paul warned us, "We preach not ourselves, but Christ Jesus the Lord"

(2 Cor. 4:5). He said to the Corinthians, "I determined not to know any thing among you, save Jesus Christ, and him crucified" (1 Cor. 2:2). But have you ever considered what considerable items of knowledge these are? To know Christ is ultimately to know all the reality and truth there is to be known, and to know the meaning of the crucifixion is to know the deepest mystery in the heart of God.

When Paul said to the Corinthians, "I determined not to know any thing among you, save Jesus Christ," he did not mean that he was going to hand to those cultivated but hardened pagans a sentimental statement about the Man of Nazareth. He did not mean that he was going to laud and magnify the name of Jesus without telling them what this meant in their relationships with one another. Did not the remainder of his letter address itself to the most embarrassing of personal problems: meat sold in the marketplaces, mixed marriages, intercourse with heathen neighbors, the abuse of the Lord's Supper, the misuse of spiritual gifts, and divisions in the church which only Christ could heal? How could they ignore such matters in the presence of Christ?

A Gospel of Grace

Paul pointed men to Christ with the hope that his healing presence might be with them. He never saw Jesus as a stern, forbidding figure but as a man in whose eyes was a deep, urgent compassion for people and in whose voice there was music and welcome. Hear him say: "Come unto me, all ye that labour and are heavy laden, and I will give you rest. Take my yoke upon you, and learn of me; for I am meek and lowly in heart: and ye shall find rest unto your souls. For my yoke is easy, and my burden is light" (Matt. 11:28–30).

Jesus is always a gentleman. He will not coerce nor force the lock nor batter down the door. Rather does he say, with quiet, holy confidence: "Behold, I stand at the door, and knock: if any man hear my voice, and open the door, I will come in to him, and will sup with him, and he with me" (Rev. 3:20). He offers to all the banquet of his grace.

A Gospel of Cheer

There were those religious leaders in the days of his flesh who said, "You cannot be very religious. You are not sad enough. Why do not you and your disciples fast as John and his disciples?" Jesus answered, "We have no cause for fasting. My ministry is like a joyous wedding week in which men are caught up in the rapture and ecstasy of celebrating the happiness of their friends. Yet, the time will come when my followers will fast. I will be taken from them and my going will be as shocking as the death of a bridegroom on the eve of his wedding. Yet, even this will not be all sadness" (cf. Matt. 9:14–15). Therefore, it was said of him, "Who for the joy that was set before him endured the cross, despising the shame, and is set down at the right hand of the throne of God" (Heb. 12:2). Then, beyond that would lie the joy of the banquet of God's grace forever, of which every man would want to be a partaker.

We are heralds of this kind of gospel. Paul's prescription for helpful preaching is this: "He who prophesies addresses men in words that edify, encourage, and console them" (1 Cor. 14:3, Moffatt).

First, preaching that puts people back together must do something for the preacher himself. Dr. John Oman once said that he did not have the slightest idea of what makes preaching popular, yet he had a pretty clear idea of what makes it edifying. It is what a man is saying to his own soul as well as to the souls of others. In this way, a Sunday may be for the minister himself a day of refreshing from the

Lord. Otherwise, it is an impoverishing as well as a dull drudgery.

We must worship with our people and not just conduct services for them. Unless the sermon enriches the spiritual life of the preacher, there is very little chance that it will strengthen others.

Preaching Should Encourage

Preaching must also encourage people. It is said that an old Negro man once came out of the counseling chamber of Dr. Harry Emerson Fosdick, his face aglow with an unearthly radiance. He told the secretary that Dr. Fosdick had put all the stars back into his sky.

Edmund Burke was one of the greatest orators of the eighteenth century. He risked and lost the political ascendancy to which he aspired because he stood for every unpopular cause you can imagine, including the cause of the American colonies. He was never the Prime Minister of England. Yet he was something greater. Someone said of him that if one stood under a doorway with Edmund Burke to escape a passing shower, one went away with one's shoulders thrown back and with heart uplifted to face the realities and battles of life.

After hearing a prominent American preacher, a man left the church saying that he made him feel strong. Preaching should always put courage back into the soul. During the blitz in England, a physician served as a true prophet as he posted a prescription for courage in the various air raid and bomb shelters. He said that it never failed to put heart into the people. It was a message taken from the third chapter of the book of Proverbs: "When thou liest down, thou shalt not be afraid: yea, thou shalt lie down, and thy sleep shall be sweet. Be not afraid of sudden fear, neither of the desolation of the wicked, when it cometh, for the Lord shall be thy confidence, and shall keep thy foot from being taken" (vv. 24–26).

Preaching then, said Paul, must console or strengthen people. To those people who had known massive pain and heavy loss, the writer of Revelation heard the living Christ say a heartening word that put power into his people: "Be watchful, and strengthen the things which remain" (3:2). To strengthen people they must be shown the invisible resources, the unseen allies which God provides. An ancient prophet once prayed a prayer that can become the prayer of the preacher as he ascends the pulpit each Sunday. The prophet was Elisha.

As he and his servant went out of the city one morning, they saw a host with horses and chariots around the city. The servant was panic-stricken and cried, "Alas, my master! how shall we do?" But the prophet reassured him by saying, "Fear not: for they that be with us are more than they that be with them" (2 Kings 6:15–16). And then Elisha prayed, "Lord, I pray thee, open his eyes, that he may see," and with that the young man saw that invisible resources attended them; the whole mountain was full of "horses and chariots of fire" (v. 17).

It is our privilege to help people see what they only dimly see, to feel what they only faintly feel, and to want what they only halfheartedly want. If we are to console people, we must go where they are. Phillips Brooks said that two things are required of a preacher: love of truth and love of souls. If we are going to learn the truth, we must make time for solitude. Goethe said that genius breeds itself in solitude, character in life's troubled sea. We must wrestle with the angel of truth alone. Yet, truth has no value unless it is expressed in the busy haunts of men.

Preaching which will strengthen and put courage and consolation in the soul must, first of all, have produced these fruits in the preacher's soul. Our gospel is always greater than any product we can fully display in our own lives, yet, our hearers have a right to expect some resemblance between the preacher's attitude and conduct and what he proclaims on Sunday.

A Tough Gospel

Preaching that helps people must be full of good cheer. We cannot represent the man who went about calling his disciples to cheer up unless we are pleasant in the pulpit. Saul and Jonathan were paid a high tribute when it was said, "Saul and Jonathan were lovely and pleasant in their lives" (2 Sam. 1:23). Every preacher carries the burden of the Lord. But the burden must be carried and not permitted to break his spirit. Our speech must be pleasant if we are to have a hearing. So often we think we are sincere only when we are scowling and conscientious only when we are scolding. Geniality is a great sweetener of life in the pulpit as elsewhere. Unless even our challenging and rebuking are seasoned with geniality, we succeed only in driving people from us.

To keep a struggling congregation above the black waters is never easy and perhaps it is never so difficult as now. Physical toughness and buoyant spirits are great assets for meeting trouble. There are many difficult people to whom you must minister, and there will be days when your health is uncertain and your heart is sad, days when you will be less fresh, less spontaneous, less fruitful in ideas. The wearisome burden will cause you to worry and will break your spirit if you are not constantly refreshed from above.

Remember, worry is not work. It is friction. It often leads

to self-pity and self-pity is slow suicide. Few things so quickly disqualify us for the ministry as self-pity. Above all, you must never parade your self-pity in public. Lord Beaconsfield once gave good advice to public speakers when he told them that no one should ever complain or explain, especially from the pulpit.

Healthy preaching is not self-conscious. Jesus did not bemoan his pathetic plight. Only once is there a passage in the Scriptures which might be so interpreted: "The foxes have holes, and the birds of the air have nests; but the Son of man hath not where to lay his head" (Matt. 8:20). There is some question here about his speaking, not of himself, but of man in general, the belief being that had he been referring to himself, he would not have contrasted himself with foxes and birds but with people. Now, Paul did speak of his suffering. He even boasted of it. Still, Paul was not at his best when he did this.

Attention should be called to the fact that Jesus never used a biographical detail. (Perhaps the parable of the vineyard was autobiography but it was still in parabolic form.) He invented his stories—of rich men, kings, and "a certain man."

Humility precludes our attempting to impress others with meritorious self-sacrifice. One of our missionaries once said, "Don't send us fellows who talk of self-sacrifice. Send us those who take danger and difficulties as the salt and pepper of life." What makes preaching attractive to the ordinary churchgoer is cheerful patience and a humility which neither asserts itself nor defers too much to human judgment.

Planned levity is seldom a fitting mood for the pulpit; neither is mock solemnity appropriate. Chaucer's "full-solemne man," who speaks in one deep, somber tone as though only the sob of the wind across a grey plateau were God's voice and never the zephyr in the smiling valley nor the tempest on the shining mountaintops, is a prime example. "A merry heart doeth good like a medicine: but a broken spirit drieth the bones" (Prov. 17:22), is sound advice for preachers.

Varied Preaching

If preaching is to help people it must be above boredom. It must have variety. It must be pleasant but it must not be that offensive, sentimental sweetness which emasculates the gospel and makes the preacher a puny caricature of the apostles. The giddy man who skips into the pulpit with an "everybody happy, say amen," is enough to make the thoughtful want to gnaw a file. His opposite is equally revolting. The morose, funereal preacher whose voice quivers under the very slightest emotion is entirely too self-conscious.

Christianity is serious but it is never sad. We who take our work most seriously need to be on our guard against two things. In our youth we are tempted to be too moralistic in our preaching. We forget that only one man in the New Testament was ever called a good man—Jesus. And Jesus repudiated the man who called him good: "Why callest thou me good? there is none good but one, that is, God" (Matt. 19:17). "Only God has perfect goodness. His goodness is never on trial. Mine is on trial every moment," said Jesus. Perhaps Jesus was not so much denying his own goodness in an absolute sense as he was repudiating the right of the spokesman to toss the word around so lightly without discerning its true meaning.

The second temptation comes to us in later life when the harp hangs silent on the willow, when health is broken, our loved ones have died, our children are gone, all the billows of life have gone over us and we are woefully depressed, we can easily pour our depression into others from the pulpit. We will then be saying, "They made me the keeper of the vineyards; but mine own vineyard have I not kept" (Song of Sol. 1:6).

We must guard our own mental and emotional health with adequate recreation, otherwise we will degenerate into abominable scolds. James Stewart once told me that scolding is the last refuge of the man who has nothing to say. Such a preacher makes goodness seem very dull and uninviting. We must be as David of old, of whom it is said in 1 Samuel: "David encouraged himself in the Lord his God" (30:6). When we are disheartened and our resilience is low and the blackness of midnight closes in about us, if we cannot encourage ourselves in the Lord our God, we have no gospel to preach.

Popular Preaching

May I also make an appeal for popular preaching? The gaudy, spectacular spellbinder, of course, obscures the gospel and is guilty of unspeakable disloyalty to his calling. But if we are to preach in a manner that helps people, we must not be too sophisticated to be popular. Of our Lord it was said, "The common people heard him gladly" (Mark 12:37). We want our people to hear us gladly also.

William Cowper depicted certain preachers whose shoddy sermons betrayed the dignity of their calling and brought the gospel into contempt. He spoke of them as

> The things that mount the rostrum with a skip,
>   And then skip down again; pronounce a text;
> Cry—hem! and reading what they never wrote,
>   Just fifteen minutes, huddle up their work
> And with a well-bred whisper, close the scene! [1]

As you stand then on the "slippery floor of a popular pulpit"—to use a phrase of Alexander Whyte's—be doubly on your guard. To be popular does not mean that you are not to go deep. But when you draw from the deep well, you need not require the congregation to drink from the bucket nor to gnaw the rope as the bucket is going down.

It is our task to speak clearly of some commonplace experience of every day. Alfred North Whitehead, in his *Adventures of Ideas*, has written, in essence, that that religion will conquer which can render clear to popular understanding some eternal greatness incarnate in the passage of temporal fact.

Remember that people come to church, not to receive your theories about truth, but for help. "Since, in the wisdom of God, the world did not know God through wisdom, it pleased God through the folly of what we preach to save those who believe. . . . God chose what is foolish in the world to shame the wise, God chose what is weak in the world to shame the strong" (1 Cor. 1:21–27, RSV). If you would help people, then follow the counsel of George Craig Stewart when he said that we should always choose a big subject and not preach mousy little sermons on the circumferential things.

You must be specific. The preacher's task has been likened to a man standing at the top of a skyscraper dropping some medicine from a pipette, and hoping to hit the mouth of a passerby in the street below who needed this prescription. If you want to put the medicine in the place where it is needed, and if you want to dwell on the big subjects, stay by the Bible. This will deliver you from the peril of monotony and, at the same time, keep you as contemporary as the morning newspaper.

Every day Cain still murders Abel. Cain may have used a

cudgel and John Doe a sawed-off shotgun, but the story is the same. A man alienates the affections of a married woman today and contrives to have her husband murdered in order that he might marry her. The husband's name is not Uriah and the woman's name is not Bathsheba but the story sounds familiar. The Bible tells the whole of human tragedy and points to the only fountain of healing.

If a preacher is to help people, he must realize that he does not have eternity in which to do it. He must learn to communicate succinctly and directly. It should not require more than twenty to twenty-five minutes to help people see some aspect of Christian living so that they are drawn to it. He must learn to omit all that is extraneous. The originality of Jesus lay not so much in what he said as in what he left unsaid. Jesus knew the economy of a great artist.

Finally, let me insist that the preparation of the preacher is far more important than the preparation of his message. When asked about the difficulty of preaching, Henry Van Dyke said that it is not hard to preach but it is very hard to bring oneself to the mood where one is fit to preach.

Notes

Chapter 1

1. Joseph Fort Newton, *River of Years* (New York: J. B. Lippincott Company, 1946), pp. 177–78.

Chapter 2

1. Oscar Hammerstein II, *Lyrics* (New York: Simon and Schuster, 1949), p. 9.

Chapter 3

1. Henry Wadsworth Longfellow, *Poems with Power to Strengthen the Soul,* ed. James Mudge (Nashville: Abingdon Press, 1935), p. 93.

Chapter 4

1. "Tomorrow's Bridge," quoted by William L. Stidger, *There Are Sermons in Stories* (Nashville: Abingdon Press, 1942), p. 217.

2. Louis H. Evans, *The Kingdom Is Yours* (Westwood, New Jersey: Fleming H. Revell Company, 1952), pp. 135–36.

Chapter 8

1. John Bunyan, *The Pilgrim's Progress* (Philadelphia: John C. Winston Company, 1933), p. 38.

Chapter 9

1. Robert Browning, "Saul," *The World's Greatest Religious Poetry*, p. 125.

Chapter 10

1. Author unknown, quoted by Theodore F. Adams, *Making the Most of What Life Brings* (New York: Harper and Brothers, 1957), p. 103.

Chapter 11

1. C. S. Lewis, *Mere Christianity* (London: Collins Clear Type Press, 1952), pp. 102–103. By permission of The Macmillan Company.

Chapter 12

1. George Herbert, "The Attitude of Gratitude," *The Minister's Manual for 1961*, ed. M. K. Heicher (New York: Harper and Brothers, 1961), p. 299.

Chapter 13

1. Newton, *op. cit.*, p. 304.

Chapter 14

1. Victor Hugo, "The Age Is Great and Strong," *The World's Greatest Religious Poetry*, p. 383.

Chapter 16

1. Richard Baxter, "Lord, It Belongs Not to My Care," *Masterpieces of Religious Verse*, ed. James Dalton Morrison (New York: Harper and Brothers, 1948), no. 1421.

2. Maltbie D. Babcock, "This Is My Father's World," *Masterpieces of Religious Verse*, no. 3.

3. Alfred Lord Tennyson, "In Memoriam," *The World's Greatest Religious Poetry,* p. 201.

Chapter 17

1. William Cowper, "Preachers: The True Vs. the Insincere," *Masterpieces of Religious Verse,* no. 1646.

252 Tr
TRENTHAM, CHARLES A.
Getting On Top Of Your Troubles

252 Tr
TRENTHAM, CHARLES A.
Getting On Top Of Your Troubles